The Plain Reader

The Plain Reader

Edited by

SCOTT SAVAGE

The Ballantine Publishing Group
New York

A Ballantine Book
The Ballantine Publishing Group

The contents of this work were originally published in *Plain* magazine.

Library of Congress Cataloging-in-Publication Data
The plain reader / [edited by] Scott Savage.
p.   cm.
Essays first appeared in Plain magazine.
ISBN 0-345-41434-9 (alk. paper)
1. Simplicity.   2. Conduct of life.   3. Simplicity—Religious
aspects—Christianity.   4. Christian life.   I. Savage, Scott.
BJ1496.P59   1998
248.4—dc21   98-9737
                                                  CIP

Text design by Holly Johnson
Cover design by Ruth Ross

Manufactured in the United States of America

First Edition: May 1998

10   9   8   7   6   5   4   3

Table of Contents

Acknowledgements

I would like to thank several people who have been critically important to this project. Victoria Shoemaker of the Spieler Agency encouraged our initial spiritual leadings concerning the need for a collection of *Plain* magazine essays, and worked to find a home for *The Plain Reader*. Mary Ann Savage, my wife and *Plain*'s managing editor initiated many of the topics and coedited a number of the essays that appeared in the magazine. Loren Pierce Coleman secured and organized permissions from our authors. Ginny Faber, *The Plain Reader*'s Ballantine editor, provided much helpful guidance and shepherded the manuscript through production. Jason Zuzga ably assisted in planning the format and arrangement of the book. Olney Friends Center allowed me to work on the *Reader* in their peaceful retreat house on the Olney campus. The Foundation for Deep Ecology granted me a stipend and has provided crucial support for *Plain*. I am more generally grateful to Keith Schneider, former correspondent for *The New York Times*, who first introduced *Plain* to a national audience in a kind and responsible way.

Above all, I want to thank the author and finisher of my faith; born in a lowly stable, He lived without worldly possessions, was persecuted and murdered, and yet vanquished death itself. Whatever is glorious or good in these pages—whatever leads to everlasting life—belongs to Jesus Christ.

A Note to Readers

Royalties from the sale of *The Plain Reader* go to support the work of the Center for Plain Living, the nonprofit 501(C)(3) corporation that publishes *Plain* magazine, and Olney Friends Center, a retreat operated by the Ohio Yearly Meeting of the Religious Society of Friends (conservative).

Subscriptions to *Plain* magazine are $18 a year, payable by check or money order to PLAIN, 60805 Pigeon Point, Barnesville, OH 43713.

Foreword

BILL MCKIBBEN

Though I'd gone to church my whole life, I was out of college before I ever *really* sat down with the Bible. To make myself go slowly, I copied out the Gospels, word for word. And they hit me like a ton of bricks. This was a dangerous, subversive book. It said quite clearly that we were not designed to live the lives we were leading. "It's *not* the economy, stupid," might as well have been written across every page. And it promised, straight out, a shot of joy to anyone who could break away from the distraction that surrounds us and focus on the real.

The book you now hold in your hands should leave you with some of the same feeling, which is not surprising, since the majority of its contributors take their inspiration from the Scriptures. It is a deeply subversive document, the most subversive document I can imagine in this day and age.

And what a testimony that is to its authors. For as we approach the millennium, there is nothing harder than to be subversive. Our consumer culture can take almost any criticism and sell it. In days of yore, it might have taken months for the ragged fashions of Haight Ashbury to show up in the department stores; now, MTV can grab any inkling of a challenge before it even becomes a coherent thought and turn it into a full-blown Attitude, available for the price of a CD. We live in a world beyond taboo.

So how on earth do you wake people up? You can't yell at them;

we live in a world of screams. But maybe you can speak softly. *Plain* magazine, the lovely and sensible journal where these pieces originally appeared, has made a point of speaking softly. Whenever its editors find out that they have made an appearance on the Internet, for instance, they send a (plain old) letter saying that they think it's not the right forum for such a discussion and asking—politely— that it cease. The Second Luddite Congress, which the Center for Plain Living organized, would have been on every TV screen in the nation, except that its conveners refused to let cameras intrude.

And yet word has spread—quietly, reflectively, but powerfully. Because there is a hunger for this brand of subversion, for the life described herein. Not because it's an easy way of life, one more "improvement." But because it's a challenging way of life, one that matches the wide array of muscles, emotions, and gifts that our Creator has bestowed on us. Is it even possible that humans have been so finely and wondrously made by God (one way or another) in order that we may recline on the couch, remote control in hand? Were we really given this set of muscles for no task harder than depressing the angle of our ankle a few degrees as our cars fly up hills? Is it fulfilling to our nature as social creatures that we now spend most of our lives at second hand, experiencing each other through the TV or the computer monitor? Did we—uniquely among all creatures— receive the gift of self-restraint in order that we might ignore it entirely and continue shopping?

The inherent *attractiveness* of more sensible ways of life is one of the things that makes them so subversive. It is impossible to read Wendell Berry and not wish that you were a farmer—and a not-insignificant number of people have read him and turned back to the land. It is impossible to read David Kline and not wonder what it might be like to be Amish. One way we resist such subversive thoughts is to imagine that it takes special types of people to lead such lives, that they are superhuman, safely beyond our power.

(This is why it makes it much easier to call Mother Teresa a saint. If she is, then there's no possibility of us emulating her, and hence no need to try.) And so one of the dangerous gifts of this book is to show us it is not so. The voices herein are often funny and self-deprecating even as they are wise. Seth Hinshaw's account of taking his first step toward driving a horse and buggy, for instance, is a classic in this vein. It makes you think: I could do that. Or at least I could ride a bike.

All of this has prosaic and practical meaning, of course. I've just come home from the huge gathering in Kyoto, Japan, called to negotiate a treaty to end global warming. It was very clear, by the end of ten fractious days, that that task will dominate our political and economic life in the twenty-first century, that we will break free of fossil fuel or we will wound creation deeply. And though the politicians are completely focused on technological answers, on macro schemes, it is obvious that these will provide only part of the answer; that people will need to change their expectations, their desires, their behaviors. We will need to abandon, or at least modify, the western consumer understanding that each one of us is at the center of the world. This book, in a fashion, is a manual for undertaking that task. For *subverting your own life*. And after that, perhaps, the lives of those around you.

In an odd sense, when every taboo has fallen, then the only way to be subversive is to have more fun than other people—to fill your heart and your home with more joy and warmth and pleasure than the frantic, slightly pathetic, ersatz happiness offered by Disney and the mall and the chat room. This is a book, finally, about joy. You may despair when you read it, and then you may do something magnificent.

Introduction: A Revolution of Hearts

SCOTT SAVAGE

Let me tell you the story of Robbie, a subscriber to the magazine I edit, a very small magazine called *Plain*. *Plain* is the Amish/Quaker/Luddite publication in which *The Plain Reader* essays first appeared.

In 1996 Robbie took a bus from New Mexico to Ohio to attend an event sponsored by *Plain*. I was there, too, at what we were calling the Second Luddite Congress. (The first such Congress was held by the original Luddites of England, weavers who revolted against the early Industrial Revolution.) The modern-day Congress drew an awful lot of national and international attention, and Robbie's presence was captured in at least one press account:

> Barnesville, Ohio—Robert L——— sat quietly in the upper reaches of the balcony at the Stillwater Friends meeting-house all weekend listening intently to the speakers who shared his uneasiness with the pace of modern technology.
>
> Yesterday, as the Second Luddite Congress wound to a close, he made his decision: He would quit his job as a computer systems analyst for [Megabig Oil Company]. "It's over," he said. "I'm going to buy a farm in Oklahoma. I've talked to enough people this weekend to know I can run a farm and make it. I just can't work for an impersonal company anymore. I don't have to."

Now, you know how conferences are. They whip you into a
frenzy over the topic, whether it's Time Management or Quantum
Business Mechanics. But on the way home you dump the whole
conference folder into the nearest wastecan. But the Second Luddite
Congress was different; sort of the opposite of time management
seminars. As time passed, it tended to work its way more deeply into
the souls of the delegates. A year and a day after it ended, Robbie sat
down at his office computer and fired off the following E-mail message to his colleagues:

```
Author: Robbie L——
Date: 4/16/97 9:19 A.M.
Priority: Normal
Subject: Taking a Flying Leap into Space


Effective May 16, 1997, I am terminating my
employment with [Megabig Oil Company]. This is
my thirty days' notice.
    Jerrie and I have felt the Lord leading us
away from the Corporate Scramble for some time.
We actually ignored this urge for several
years, but only in the last year have we had an
inkling of where we were to go. We are moving
back to Oklahoma, among most of our relatives,
to locate an acreage on which to homestead.
    "Homestead," not as in the legal definition,
but as in raising our own food (plants and an-
imals) and making a life, instead of merely
making a living.

Background (for anyone who wishes to read on):
    1) Because our economic system is so orga-
```

nized, corporations must grow to survive, and the growth of thousands of organizations means the ultimate consumption of all natural resources. If this continues, there will be nothing left to pass on to our descendants. This is not what I want for my descendants, so I'm not helping to do it anymore.

2) Because our economic system forces competition, employees are constantly being pushed to run, run, run. My artistic blood and my conscience both rebel when we often seem to be fooling our customers into thinking that they are getting quality work, instead of taking time to actually give it to them.

3) What keeps our economic system going? Well, everybody in the western world wants to live like royalty; travel, fine food, nice clothes, power. To live like royalty you need a large contingent of servants fulfilling your every whim. In the old days, a few people were royalty and everyone else was their slave. In the present day, everyone is royalty (or wants to be), and machines are our slaves. This works in the short term, but will surely fail when (a) the energy runs out, or (b) the environment has become so miserable that life is a royal pain. The industrial age was a nice diversion, but Jerrie and I are getting back on track and going on to the future.

4) We are also unhappy with a social system that separates fathers from their children, and lately, mothers from their children, for a majority of the day, leaving the children's

upbringing to strangers. Homesteading and home schooling (already in progress) let us all stay at home where we need to be.

5) Sitting behind a desk day after day is killing my body. Many of you know that I constantly fight back problems. Being up and active and doing some real physical work will do tremendous things for my health. And no, I'm not planning to just sit on a tractor.

6) I fear I'm missing the majority of God's gifts by hiding out in a building my entire life. I've got to check out the other side and see how much joy I've been avoiding by not immersing myself in Creation.

We aren't making this move lightly, but only after much agonizing thought, discussion, and prayer. However, things have certainly gone right for us since we made the decision—so many things that we are certain it's God's will for us to go.

We are not waiting until I reach retirement age. We want to do this while all the kids are still at home, and while we are still young.

For the most part, I have enjoyed my time with [Megabig Oil]. I have definitely enjoyed knowing each of you, especially my colleagues in Computer Land (just south of Fantasy Land). Thanks for all the assistance with all the problems, the encouragement, and the laughs. I'm not leaving in a bitter mood, but with my eyes fixed on something that promises to be much better.

Catch me, Lord! Here I come!

At the very moment Robbie was pressing the computer key that would send his job into outer space, I was entering the capital city of Ohio on foot, fulfilling a pledge I had made (to myself) at the Congress. I had walked the 120 miles from my home in Barnesville to Columbus to cancel my driving privileges.

These are cautionary tales; who would quit a perfectly good job to become a subsistence farmer? Why would anyone want to give back to the state the right to drive a car?

Maybe you'll understand better after reading *The Plain Reader*. Perhaps, in light of these essays, it will make sense that the first *New York Times* reporter who came to see *Plain* magazine quit his job two weeks later and started a grassroots movement to protect western Michigan from the oil and gas industry. Dozens of similar narratives of drastic and fantastic life changes arrive in the weekly mail, attesting to *Plain*'s tiny, but lethal, roar against the status quo.

Plain was launched a few years ago by the nonprofit Center for Plain Living, a small band of mostly Quaker plain people who wanted to be a bridge between the Anabaptist and Friends traditions—what are sometimes called the Believers or Peace churches—and the rest of society. The magazine came about because my wife and Center for Plain Living cofounder Mary Ann Savage (pen name: Mary Ann Lieser) and I couldn't find much discussion in the print media concerning all the incredible discoveries we were making on the road to a simpler life. We had gotten to the point where it seemed as if we were living in a different country from the journalists, when we compared what was being written and talked about with what really mattered to us.

While the popular press was scratching its head over a health care system whose costs had spun completely out of control, and whose outcomes routinely put it at the very bottom of the list of industrialized nations, we were having our babies born at home with a midwife, and learning the health benefits of herbs and good nutrition. While huge blue-ribbon panels of experts published multivolume critiques of our dysfunctional government-run schools, we became a family of dropouts, learning at home. As the media culture reached for O.J. and Paula Jones and Tim McVeigh, we threw away everything electronic and started spending our time with Jesus. We were a family that had slowly come to live in a fully realized, sustainable culture that is largely invisible to modern society. We'd gone plain.

Plain became a means for the people of this alternative world to relate their experiences. The magazine's circulation quickly grew to a self-sustaining level of five thousand subscribers (I edit probably the only magazine that ever *turned away* subscribers to stay small). Physical production of *Plain* has progressed—backward—to the precomputer age, just to show it can be done. Every page of *Plain* is composed of hand-set type and original woodcuts, printed on a hand-fed, solar-powered antique press. At our slow, quiet pace, we have replaced the computers with people, instead of the other way around. The result has been an enhanced level of caring, the essence of good work. And the compelling nature of the essays in *Plain* is complemented by the fact that we have woven the words together by hand, like a basket full of something wise and good that is then sent out into the world. Our sincerest intention is to be a catalyst for changing lives, the success of which many of our readers attest to.

Why, you might ask, are these hand-printed essays on simple, low-tech, and spirit-filled living so convincing? I think it must be because they are so truthful, the honest and personal stories of people who speak from experience.

This is an unusual approach for a magazine to take in an age when the question of how we should live is theorized, expertized, and criticized several times over before the next commercial break, all to no end. It is as if we have talked and talked ourselves into the unconscious certainty that improving our society is actually impossible. The feeling of hopelessness engendered by this remains unshaken by even the most dire warnings of social activists. In fact, hearing of the danger of the moment only serves to paralyze most of us. As Elmo Stoll points out in his essay "Better than Fixing Things" (p. 175):

> It seems as though the entire world is on board a train that is speeding rapidly downhill, picking up momentum all the time, and although many are dismayed at the direction they are traveling, they seemingly can find no way to safely jump off.

This book is an antidote to the feeling that our choices are nil. The writers have a great message to share: Yes, if you stop talking to answering machines and digital robots, or if you unplug your television, or if you start buying locally grown food, or if you even go so far as to quit your job to return to your family and community—take just one courageous step back from the downhill plunge of modern life—you will be rewarded with some wonderful, unforeseeable gifts, one of which is the gift of choice.

In my life I choose to follow Christ. The path that most fully supports my faith is the path of Quakerism in its most conservative mold. The decisions I make about my existence here on Earth—to live simply, dress plainly, travel slowly, and to do good work—these are my imperfect attempts to submit to the will of God. So, in a sense I have chosen *not* to choose, at least not to let the choice be merely my own or that of my fellow countrymen. Through my religious group, my reading of Scripture, and my direct experience of the Holy Spirit, I am submitting to the only power I know who can deliver everlasting meaning to life.

Choosing to have a spiritually led life informs my daily decisions. The forms these incidental choices take can end up changing me, as well. Because I write with pencil and paper and typewriter (in order to do things simply), I am exposed to a different, more linear way of developing thought than when using a word processor.

This, in turn, influences how I think in general, an unforeseen consequence!

Choosing our tools is part of the essence of plainness. Amish folk don't drive horse and buggies because, as one computer scientist tried to convince me, they are "late adopters" of technology. They do it because they want to avoid the social problems caused by auto ownership. Mary Ann makes the same case in her "Deleting Childhood" essay on page 226 when she declares, "I believe that computers are not just a tool we use for good or ill, as the case may be. Computers use us, too." John Taylor Gatto is saying it in "What Really Matters" on page 212:

> Everyone who winds life around a core of machinery— physical machinery or social machinery, like schools and institutions and global corporations—is affected profoundly, and comes inexorably, I believe, to be a servomechanism of the machinery he or she excessively associates with.

People who live beyond the reach of the machinery of modern life—the technosphere that increasingly invades every corner of existence—are our only reminders of what living is really all about. They recall for us its sacred character. The mere presence in the midst of the consumer society of communities in which full, authentic, and meaningful lives are the norm is both startling and miraculous.

We have reached the point where the technosphere's machinery for providing comfort and amusement has largely replaced the power and complexity of the natural world, at least in our immediate experience. People have tended to resist the onslaught by wishing for a return to simple living. This desire for front porches and apple trees and happy old grandpas sipping lemonade is well understood in the media marketplace, which happily co-opts such longings.

Wendell Berry, whose essay "Health Is Membership" appears on page 49, once told me, however, that *he* wasn't attempting to live more simply, he was trying to live *more complexly*. This was a reminder that beyond any slogans of the marketplace, living outside our megatech world of comfort and convenience involves more personal relationships, more responsibility, more *giving* than most of us are used to. Leaving it all behind to live the simple life really means relearning all the very detailed and specific needs of the people, places, and things we care about. The technosphere quite openly defines itself as the champion of individuality and self-interest. But living complexly means embracing wholeness, and committing to it, rather than seeking an individual solution—however "simple." Simplicity practiced in isolation is not the key to our survival.

The technosphere has a well-documented history of threatening not only the well-being of our places (what the media vaguely define as *the environment*) but also the health of human communities and cultures. The industrial nations and their transnational companies are creating a global economy that appears to be causing an ecological collapse—but we are being collapsed, as well. Indigenous, ethnic, religious, and rural cultures and communities are disappearing, not with the advance of occupying armies, but with the advance of McDonald's restaurants and satellite television.

We can only expect that this march toward conformity will intensify. John Perry Barlow of the Electronic Frontier Foundation tells us:

We are all going there, whether we want to or not. . . . When we are all together in cyberspace we will see what the human spirit and the basic desire to connect can create there. I am convinced that the result will be more benign if we go there open-minded, openhearted, and excited with the adventure than if we are dragged into exile.

I would add only that in a sense we have already gone "there" into cyberspace, because the technosphere already surrounds us with a virtual reality of limitless consumption and infinite amusement. The term *virtual*, however, means *not quite*, and the virtual life offered by modern society is not quite what it seems.

Jesus asked the crowd, "Who among you, if his son asks for bread, will give him a stone?" But the technosphere not only offers us stones, it insists they are bread: virtual reality; virtual community; godlike powers of mobility and wealth (supported by nonrenewable energy); a gospel of perfect health and eternal youth that robs our preparations for inevitable sickness and death.

One hope offered by several essayists in *The Plain Reader* is that we can begin to rebirth communities that value smallness, localness, and face-to-face contact. The Amish might be seen as examples of such communities functioning today. However, as writers such as Wendell Berry and Art Gish are quick to remind us, communities like the Amish which have withstood the pressure of modern life are not mere collections of individuals who happen to share a dislike for the materialistic present. It is *only* because they view human nature as fallen—a distinctly nonmodern belief—that the Amish have successfully resisted the more vile aspects of American life. Having acknowledged their own incompleteness, they are humbled and brought together. The Amish word for community means *brotherhood*. And they have taken steps as a community—a religious body—to be rescued from their admitted imperfections.

Humility of this sort offers the greatest threat to the continued dominance of the technosphere, consumer culture, hedonistico-bureaucracy—whatever you want to call modern life. Knowing that no thing, no consumable or lifestyle or media event can make us whole is a very good starting point.

A quiet underpinning of much of what you will find in *The Plain*

Reader is the idea that we will naturally overthrow the reign of consumption in our lives when we reconnect with God. As the editor of *Plain*, I've seen that this is one of the hardest lessons for our readers to accept, even as they seek a higher truth. The people of my generation have been raised with the counterculture's judgment that monotheism and western hegemony are one and the same.

But that is not my religion, which speaks to me instead of the fact that the earth is the Lord's, and the fullness thereof. In the circles of Christianity within which I travel, many believers have been imprisoned and even murdered for their insistence on being faithful, on treating every person as equally loved by God. My church resists evil with love and with the very lives of its adherents.

During the opening session of the Second Luddite Congress, a man in a plain straw hat shocked some of the delegates by explaining the real truth behind our resistance to modernity. The Christian communitarian Art Gish smiled into the faces of several hundred activists, ecologists, and spiritual seekers—and deflated the cause that had brought them all together:

> It is important to remember that Luddism is not the answer. The answer is not in saving the earth. We can't save the earth. The answer is not in rejecting technology. There is something more important than getting rid of oppressive technology.
>
> The answer of Jesus is to seek first God's kingdom, and then all these things will find their proper perspective. . . . This biblical view naturally leads us to a life of nonconformity to the old, sick society, to the creation of a counterculture. It leads to a life of resistance to the principalities and power of oppression. Isn't that what we want? A counterculture that will provide an alternative to virtual reality.

Does providing an alternative to the technosphere amount to creating a social protest movement? Recent experience warns us away from structured protest, I believe. The global marketplace has shown an enormous appetite for cultural artifacts of all stripes, which it repackages for sale as commodities. It matters not whether these initial expressions of human energy and creativity support or criticize the marketplace itself; everything is grist for the mill. If the voluntary simplicity movement has become a trend, then the trend sniffers of the marketplace are surely busily at work co-opting voluntary simplicity. The technosphere eats social protest movements for breakfast.

These lessons indicate that it is useless to exert force against the modern paradigm, even the force of ideas. The electronic media in particular thrives on such outputs of human energy. Which is not to suggest that we say nothing, or that there is nothing to be done. Rather, we need to realize that it is useless to employ tactics of mass action and propaganda, which do nothing to weaken the hold of the "old, sick society." The clue as to what we *can* do is found in the technospheric message itself, the underlying untruth repeated over and over: "There is no turning back; you have no choice." We have been struck dumb by this message of hopelessness. What would happen if we refused to believe it? What would happen if we *said* as much, one on one, to the people around us?

With hope comes the sudden recognition that we can easily weaken the hold of this machine around which our lives are so tightly wound, *merely by pulling the plug*. We can stop feeding the technosphere our energy by severing our ties to it.

I know, because I've done it. As soon as I issued a blanket refusal to listen, look at, or buy from the culture of modernity, it began to lose its power over my behavior and my thinking. And that also meant that its overall power diminished by one "person-unit" of energy. Best of all, my resistance could not be co-opted or channeled into buying something, *because I could no longer be reached*.

Each time any person makes this kind of refusal, the overall strength of materialism and invasive technology is reduced, because its power comes entirely from us. The Amish, who are loathe to judge others, nevertheless have told me many times that it is plain to them that people in the larger society are not just victims of the machine. They are making the machine go.

I wish I could say that the process of resisting is always pleasant. My own experience at first was to discover the things I lacked and had not known I needed—like a real community and a culture of spiritual maturity. Where was I going to find all that? Ever since this initial feeling of not knowing where to start, however, I have been continually struck by the amazing number of new choices offered when I trusted God to help me hop off the downhill speeding train:

I have real relationships with people, with all the abundant life of nature that surrounds me, and with God. I don't have any virtual relationships with television shows, sports personalities, or radio talk show hosts.

I refuse to behave or be labeled as a consumer or any other object. Of course, I hang up on answering machines and always tell the long-distance telephone information robot that I must speak with a human being.

My tastes have become unjaded, so I can actually experience the simple and good things in life I used to hear so much about.

I have hope. For me, life is meaningful. I know that good wins in the end, so I'm not as full of anxiety, agitation, or depression as was once the case.

If you're skeptical that these benefits really come from living the unplugged life, I can understand. Similar testimonials show up in the media all the time from people whose lives have been changed by eating miracle health foods, or watching *Star Trek* reruns. My experience, and that of the essayists in *The Plain Reader*, are just examples meant for encouragement. They aren't prescriptions for achieving perfection.

I would hope that even if you are heavily invested in the technosphere, and as cynical as all get-out about the prospects of leaving it, you will still let the *Reader* speak to you a little bit. Don't feel judged by our critiques.

It might even be helpful to consider "de-investing" from some part of the machine world for a while, just to see if your perceptions change. Would it be possible to stop using your workplace computer for a week (or a month!), finding other ways temporarily to complete your work? Maybe you could visit a library, page through a career guide, and imagine yourself safely, *happily* making a living without a machine interface. Put your TV in the closet for a while. Walk or ride a bike to work if that's possible. Then come back to *The Plain Reader* and see if these essays are starting to make sense.

If some part of *The Plain Reader* encourages you to take that first step, what a wonderful thing that would be. At least let the voices herein tell their stories, tales you'll never hear on television or see over the Internet.

Welcome to a hope-filled world. Please share this book with others. If you see it—tucked under an arm at the other end of a room—go on over and introduce yourself as a reader of the *Reader*, too. That is, after all, the most appropriate way to spread the news of this strange, alternative, upside-down world of horse-driven carriages, televisionless houses, and family-size gardens: by greeting strangers one on one. It is my hope that we will all come to realize, on closer inspection, that the world of *The Plain Reader* is right-side up.

And yes, yes, you can turn back.

Making a Life

How is it that making a living has replaced making a life? We'll never find out by following the tangle of issues that rage around this question. Do we need better child care options so that every able-bodied adult is employed in the formal economy? Or should we recognize the call of political conservatives to return to the "traditional" family? It is a hollow debate, destined to go round and round, because it avoids definitions. What if the very concept (and reality) of employment isn't some automatic good, but rather something about which we have no choice? What if the opposite of having a job isn't unemployment, but rather producing for our own needs?

What if the "traditional" family isn't husbands at jobs and wives watching soap operas? What would you say if I told you I don't want women to stay at home, I want to welcome everyone to come back home? Where we all were before the Industrial Revolution or the global economy. David and Elizabeth Vendley have made that journey from the world of working for a living—commuting suburbanites who went looking for some definitions of what work is for—and ended up joining the Amish. When it comes to making a life, they have the idea that home can be the base of our productivity: "Homemade everything, from dresses to cereal to noodles."

Making a life is also striking a blow for freedom. In the opening sessions of the Second Luddite Congress, hundreds of delegates took up the question of how our society can begin to change again after decades of stasis, torrents of fruitless debate. Amish farmer and nature writer David Kline spoke to us of the essential need for kindness, mutual aid, and community to free us from the captivity of "employment." And firebrand contrary farmer Gene Logsdon passed on the essential secret of late-twentieth-century guerrilla warfare: "You can't stop a monopolistic egg factory under the present economic dictatorship. But you can start raising your own eggs."

Everyone who attended the Second Luddite Congress was considered a delegate. Imagine yourself seated on a bench in the 120-year-old Stillwater Friends meetinghouse, surrounded by people of all backgrounds gathered together. One by one, they rise to speak their hearts to the assembly.

Seeking Personal Freedom in a Money Dictatorship: An Address to the Second Luddite Congress

GENE LOGSDON

I don't know if I can address my worries about technology without hypocrisy or inconsistency. It is clear to me that, broadly speaking, technology is part of life. The gull that flies high in the air and drops a clam on the rocks to break it uses technology. A northern oriole's nest is an exquisite example of technology.

On a human level, I am grateful that technology has provided us with toilet paper.

I dislike automobiles and would not feel much deprivation if I never had to ride in one again. But I would not be here at the Second Luddite Congress if cars did not exist. Of course, if cars did not exist, I doubt there would have been any reason for this meeting.

To be frank, I can't solve the intellectual dilemma that technology causes me. I know only that virtue is moderation in all things, and there is no moderation in technology anymore. In sports we agree to put limits on technology. We dictate how a baseball bat is to be made, how much it dare weigh. In some cases we even dictate that "over the fence" is "out." Isn't it strange that we recognize the need to limit technology in games, but not in real life? Sometimes we make feeble efforts to limit technology in other areas. We make a sixty-five-miles-an-hour speed limit and then make cars that can go one hundred. Does that make sense?

We are never satisfied with our technology. The first computers were as big as a house. Now we have some as small as a mouse. The technologists boast about putting more and more information on smaller and smaller chips while they brag about putting more and more horsepower into bigger and bigger tractors. How much more information will we cram onto a computer chip before we are satisfied? How much faster will we be able to fly to Europe before we are satisfied? Till we get there before we start? How much bigger can a tractor get? I keep thinking, well, now surely we have reached the limit. Surely if we try to go one step farther, we'll fall flat on our technological face, or fall off some technological cliff and crash.

I know a farmer who keeps on buying farmland until he has more than he can handle even with the biggest tractors. He rents it out to other farmers. But he is already terribly rich. Why must he keep on hogging more land? Is the technology at fault or is it plain old human nature being unable to practice moderation in all things? Is the technology at fault or is it human nature at fault? I think about that a lot, but I can't think of an answer that satisfies me completely.

An unlimited technology gives the lust for power a chance to operate without limits, too. Dictatorships thrive when technological power is unlimited. Can you imagine a Robin Hood being able to hide out today in Sherwood Forest even if there was a Sherwood Forest to hide in?

But the dictatorship that threatens to enslave us today is of a more insidious kind than political or military despotism. We are caught in a spider's web of economic dictatorship. Political dictators are easily recognized. Corporate dictators are not. Using the unlimited power of informational technology in advertising, in schooling, in television dramas, the money god appears before us as an indulgent friend, convincing us that it is all we need for happiness. Everything desirable is for sale.

Money has always been a powerful allurement, but can anyone doubt that today money rules our lives as never before? My great-grandfather took an ax and a cow to the land where I now live and established the kind of life he wanted and that he could not find in Germany. Who can do that today? Today it is very difficult to listen to a different drummer, to refuse to join the rat race, to be content with a modest house and a modest income for the reward of living in the place and in the way one wants to live.

Insurance and taxes and inflation alone make the modest way of life almost unaffordable. The pursuit of money drives working people, blue collar and white collar, to such long hours working for others, that there is neither spare time nor opportunity to produce part of one's living at home, outside of the money loop. So the job becomes God, becomes everything, and we are held to it by the need to buy what we might in another situation produce ourselves. We become chained to that job like a galley slave chained to his oar. There is no life beyond the job except for a fleeting vacation and fleeting luxuries on which we spend the savings that might have eventually bought us a little freedom.

I'm not talking specifically about saying no to computers, to cars, to airplanes, to tractors, to genetic engineering. I'm talking about parents who feel forced to put very young children in day care centers not so much because they need to work for cash, but because they need jobs to afford the horrendous cost of adequate medical coverage.

I'm talking about being forced to pay for a schooling system that treats children as if they were robots to be programmed to become money spenders so that they will be able to pay the political dictator plenty of taxes and spend the rest keeping the corporate dictators wealthy.

I'm talking about waking up in the morning, as some of us have in Ohio, to find that the largest egg factory in the world is being built beside our farms, not only threatening the economy of small farms, but violating the very air and water and space in which we live. There is no shortage of eggs, no need at all for this factory. It is being built solely because it is technologically possible for one operation to raise as many eggs as the whole state of Ohio does now. It is in fact nothing more than an act of economic aggression to corner the egg market in this state.

I'm talking about waking up in the morning and learning that a new and unnecessary highway is coming right through the middle of your farm. When a farmer in our county learned about this, he died of a heart attack within twenty-four hours.

The lust for power will always be with us, like the poor. I see no solution. In any individual time in history you wish to study, greed wins most of the battles. But goodness always endures the war, picks up the pieces, goes on to endure the next greed war.

Because of my fatalistic attitude, I don't see any way to stop the dreadnought of technologically greased machinations of power until they collapse of their own bloat. I prefer to cope with the situation by personal action, not by philosophizing or by political movement. I do not shun technology. I use it on a low level to fight those on the high level who use it to try to gain power over me.

If information highways are the wave of the future, then I will build information country roads on which the traveler can reach the truth faster by going slower. If the economic dictators use technology to gain a monopoly in the food business, as they are absolutely trying to do, then I will use technology to show how a society of garden farmers can start a new home economy that will confound the dictators. You can't stop a monopolistic egg factory under the present economic dictatorship. But you can start raising your own eggs. If enough of us do it, not to make money, but to feed ourselves, the power of the food monopolies will be broken.

And so I write. Book after book. I write about what many of us are doing to establish a new home-based society with a stable economy mostly free of the greed economy. I believe that if just 25 percent of the people in this country would turn to this kind of life, this cautious use of technology to elevate the individual, to decentralize the marketplace, then we could as a society return to a more democratic and therefore healthy economy.

My goal is only to live this way myself because it is such a lovely way to live, and to inform those others who have the same yearnings as I have, but perhaps have never had their eyes opened to the possibilities. No better time than now to start. Downsizing is accelerating this development. The low qualities of factory food are compelling it. The high cost and harassment of recreation away from home encourages it.

People ask me, what can they do? I say to one and all, buy a little land and get it paid for. An acre could be enough, but five are better. Twenty are better yet. Get a little land before the monopolists take it. If you love that land, living on it and taking care of it, wonderful things can happen for you.

Community:
An Address to the Second Luddite Congress

DAVID KLINE

It has been said that community is like an old coat: you aren't aware of it until it is taken away. This is where I probably differ from many of you here. I was born and raised in a low-tech agrarian community, looked outward, and yes, I yearned for more technology. You are more likely to be coming from the outside world and are traveling—or at least looking—toward a less materialistic, stronger sense of community.

I became aware of what community is when I was drafted during the Vietnam War and served two years working in a hospital in a big city. My plain Amish coat was taken away. But that is getting ahead of my story.

(I must confess I'm not as well prepared for this talk as I hoped to be. We were plowing yesterday, and I had planned to do my writing while the horses rested between rounds. But then we got company. A young man from Kansas, a long-distance truck driver who had delivered a load to Cleveland, stopped by our farm on his way home. Parking his 18-wheeler along the road, he "helped" me plow. Since I was using the walking plow he walked with me. I listened to how his grandfather in Minnesota had farmed with horses and heard about his own aspirations of getting off that truck and on his own farm, where he wants to milk a herd of fine Brown Swiss cows. I hope his dream comes true.)

Ralph Waldo Emerson wrote that a man standing in his own

field is unable to see it. I think that was the case with me growing up; I had my nose too close to the picture.

That changed somewhat when I was about twelve years old. During the Eisenhower presidency and the USDA's Soil Bank days, the government told the farmers how many acres of wheat they could grow.

In order to verify farmer compliance, the government sent a technician out to measure the field. If there was too much wheat, it had to be cut for hay or ensiled. When the young technician visited our farm he had a large aerial photograph of the entire neighborhood, which he spread out on the hood of his car. Dad then showed him which field was sown in wheat.

I looked at the map and marveled at the landscape from the air—the view the red-tailed hawk had when it soared high over the fields. There, meandering through the pasture field, was the creek where we fished and skinny-dipped. And the woods with all its interesting creatures. There was the one-room schoolhouse with its massive white oak by the front entrance and red oak next to the baseball backstop. I could already smell the freshly oiled wood floor and looked forward with anticipation to September when the new school year would begin. Because it was there on those three acres that the study of nature and creation and language and music and arithmetic and softball became one.

From that photograph my horizons broadened. But it was when I moved to the city to start my Vietnam War conscientious objector service that I began to realize what community is all about.

I started work in November of that year, and within a month it snowed. Going to my landlady's garage, I found a snow shovel and started cleaning off her sidewalk along the street. Ah, this was more like farmwork again, hands-on labor! I got carried away and shoveled off the snow several houses down and up the street. When I returned to the house, my landlady was extremely upset.

"Why?" I asked.

"You cleaned off Mrs.————'s sidewalk . . . and I don't like her."

I wised up in a hurry. Not only did the people dress differently in the city, they thought differently, too.

When I had left the farm for the city, I thought I might not return. Maybe I would gravitate toward a higher-tech life. But I did return to the farm where, as Bill McKibben writes, "humus and human meet." Where, instead of *Peyton Place*, I watched orioles and butterflies and listened to what the land had to teach.

I returned to a community that chooses to work with their hands, believing manual labor is close to godliness. A community where technology is restricted and "book learning" is frowned upon. Where even the hymns are passed down without the notes being written down. In this culture, you learn from a master. There is always someone who possesses the arts and skills you need.

I soon noticed on returning home that my role models were local people, neighbors instead of entertainment celebrities. My uncle, who lived on the next farm and was a voracious reader, enthralled me with dog stories—*The Little Shepherd of Kingdom Come* and *The Voice of Bugle Ann*.

Another neighbor, a fine horseman, taught me a great deal about handling and loving the gentle draft horse. When he lost his larynx to cancer (no, he didn't smoke) his horses responded to his slightest touch of the lines and he continued to farm.

Most of these role models are now resting in hillside cemeteries on farms throughout the neighborhood. I often hear that our people came to America (on the invitation of the Quaker William Penn) for religious freedom. Which is true, but they also came to have their own farms. Practically all of the first settlers are buried on the land they tilled, on the land that nurtured them and their families.

Of course, growing up with horse farming and staying with animal traction when the rest of society switched to fossil-fuel traction didn't go unnoticed by us younger boys. We had never heard of Ned Lud and we would say to Dad, "Dad, if we would get rid of these horses, we could milk ten more cows."

His response was always the same: "But then we wouldn't have all that good horse manure, and besides, tractors compact the soil."

If we Amish in northeastern Ohio look at our community and all its small villages that are thriving—Berlin, Mount Hope, Charm, Farmerstown, Fredericksburg, Kidron—in spite of a Wal-Mart ten miles away, we can see it is because of the horse. Seldom do we travel farther than five or six miles to a small town to do our business. Some may go to Wal-Mart but not on a weekly basis. The standardbred horse helps us, even if we think globally, to act locally.

These small towns and their markets benefit the outlying counties. A while back I took some eggs to the weekly auction in Mount Hope. As I carried them in I noticed a car with its trunk open and an elderly farmer lifting out a case of eggs. The license plate was from several counties west of us. Why, I thought, do they have to bring their eggs all this way to flood our market?

Then I realized that their small towns and markets are gone, and my heart softened.

Welcome, friend, we are delighted to have you here.

Right at Home

DAVID AND ELIZABETH VENDLEY

Home. Is yours what you want it to be? Ours was not. We were not in control; our standards were constantly being influenced by society. It was a place of compromise and little backbone. There seemed to be quite a bit of competition for our lifestyle decisions: magazines and newspapers, television and Hollywood, the advertising and fashion industries, the public school system, just to name a few. By the time all of these have their way with a home, the family structure consecrated by God begins to fall.

For a "free" country, we sure are easily captivated by these influences. Well, that is what freedom is, one would suppose, but freedom is also the ability *not* to follow these influences. Freedom *from*. Our house needed *freedom from* a lot more than *freedom to*. The world uses media, peer status, technology, and financial wealth as their guideposts. We, however, switched to a different measuring stick, namely the Bible. For our family, this was a change from how it was when we first married.

We would have been considered an average American consumer family at one time, consuming what we wanted as well as what we needed, seeking our own welfare rather than our brother's. Both being from professing Christian families, we had set up a typical church-going household, mostly as a customary practice. We are now Amish, not by birth, however, but by choice. The deep spiritual reasons and benefits are too vast and personal to be covered here, but we would like to address the various facets of this transition as it has affected the functions of our household.

As plain people we have a scriptural calling to separate from the world. We do this because we feel as if we are "renters" here, husbandmen of sorts who will most definitely have to give account for the stewardship we exercise until that happy, happy day comes when we return home to the Savior. Bearing this in mind we soberly move forward, making lifestyle choices for our family.

The first area for us was clothing. Although never really fashion bugs, we were dependent on the stores and their designers for our clothing options. We often felt frustrated by these limitations; the store clothing often lacked taste or practicality. So Mom learned to

sew. A few memories of seventh-grade home-ec class were dusted off and generous portions of trial and error compensated for the rest. Altering store patterns, we came up with personal uniforms we were comfortable with. This process took several months (later we located a company that sold plain clothing patterns). Some peculiar things came from the sewing room in those days, but eventually we were blessed to be able to make most of our own clothes.

This freed us in several ways. It freed us from the great monster of consumerism. *We* chose our fabric, *we* chose the pattern, *we* chose the skirt lengths, shirt colors, etc. *We* were in more control. This enabled us to use our own measuring stick to set our family's dress standards. Dad now felt more in control of deciding how the family would look. We saved bunches of money since we located a reasonable fabric supplier. And once Mom worked the kinks out, we gained physical comfort due to a looser fit. We felt more stable and natural in clothing we had chosen and made ourselves. The benefits, by far, outweighed the work involved.

Another area of change for us was our food. This entailed (for economic reasons at first) gardening and extensive canning. Through books from the library and a water-bath canner received as a gift, we began. Between our garden and a weekly produce auction in the next county, the Lord made sure we had plenty. Once again the financial differences were quite large. We have sat down together and done the figures that proved our profit far outweighed the workload. We found ourselves skipping several sections of the grocery store. It became a contest to see how many aisles we could do without. We began to see how Mom's staying at home gave her time to do these things for us. She saved us as much (if not more) than she would have earned in the job market once the cost of day care, second car, wardrobe, etc., were subtracted.

Since we have moved from the suburbs to the country we can now keep small livestock for our dairy, egg, and meat needs. A few chores and butchering and we now need very little from the grocery store. All around, homemade is best for us, and we have more choices and control. We are freed all the more from consumerism.

We also pulled away from some of the world's more formal institutions. The first was media. So often we hear people berate the standards of television these days, saying they "should pull the plug, *but* . . ." Most have an excuse or exception, but we didn't. It wasn't hard to do, because there was so little fit to watch and the bad far outweighed the good. The newspaper and magazines were easy to do without, because their absence immediately freed us from pressure. There was no longer a crowd of professional opinion pushers trying to influence us. We still get the news—by word of mouth for general events. Then if we *choose*, we can investigate further from sources *we* choose. We now stand careful guard over the influences that come through our household, weighing each carefully, slowly, and personally.

The public school is another influence we have chosen to do without. It had always been obvious to us that the system of public schooling, while founded on the noblest of intentions, has digressed into little else than a place for social engineering. We did not want to struggle against their more harmful teachings all the time, lest our children misinterpret and disregard the academics that are offered in the midst of all the misguided information. The sorting job alone was a full-time adult-size chore. We are blessed with and so grateful for an alternative. We have a one-room schoolhouse operated among the neighborhood and the church. If we did not have this, we would home-school, public schooling not even being an option in our minds. We are agreed on the importance of basic education, but we are not willing to give up our own stewardship of our children's minds for six or seven hours each day.

Although we are not totally free of the medical world, we have at least reduced its influence on our lives. Again, using books, we have learned how to make some effective (and gentler) salves and remedies in order to withdraw from the pharmaceutical whirlpool. We do use the hospital for severe illness, but not for natural life conditions such as birth. Our beliefs on the God-ordained birth process lead us to regard it as an intimate life passage rather than an illness full of lurking complications. Our last two babies, by the grace of God, were born safely and gently at home with the help of a competent lay midwife. We realize that this is not always practical, or even legal in some places. However, for us, having been blessed with four uneventful hospital births, the best place for all of us was home.

In the case of home birth, the benefits so grossly outweigh the risks that a family like us hardly has to pause before choosing it. Albeit, we have had occasion to be grateful that the hospital was there for life-threatening situations. But we do feel we ought to control how much of our lives the medical world takes part in.

So much more has changed about us than the way we look or the fact that we get around by horse and buggy. We have gained a great freedom, freedom from the world and its trappings. No longer snared into doing things everyone else's way but our own, we've gained control over our household and thus surrendered it to the will of God.

Sure, we're the first to admit it's a lot of work. But what else do we have to do as we pass our days here? Chase after folly and self-pleasure? That is hardly what we understand the Scriptures to require.

Work is so thoroughly bad-mouthed in modern society that we

would do well to stop and take a commonsense look at the American view (or allergy) concerning work.

America's current love affair with technology is partly based on the notion that hard work is a bad thing. If you are the smart guy, you'll think of faster, easier ways to do things than by manual labor. The cleaner one's hands are from the grime of hard work, the more highly esteemed and highly paid. In the average factory there are usually a few fellows whose main goal is to change the color of their shirt collars from blue to white. There is usually a storehouse of tales in each family of how Grandpa toiled in the coal mines so Dad could go to college. Now we hear how Dad toils at the office so Junior can complete his homework on his personal computer in his bedroom. It is hard to imagine how much higher we can possibly build our technological Tower of Babel before it comes tumbling down.

Our question is, what's wrong with work? Nothing. It is healthy, productive, and satisfying. It is also time-consuming. We wonder when we ever found time to sit in front of the TV. But we feel our time now is well spent at manual labor rather than pleasure seeking. Work is our favorite pastime; we have just changed our goal from thrills to satisfaction and productivity. Our idea of fun is to sort potatoes or squish tomatoes in a grinder as a family. Counting jars of peaches, making a human assembly line to wash and label jars, milking goats—that's fun. Our best family memories come from experiences in two places: one when we renovated an old house, the other working in our produce patch.

Home. A powerful word. One of double meaning for a Christian. Home, of course, is the place in which we presently dwell, but home is also our ultimate goal, Heaven. For our family, our true home is that place of rest with our Savior, Jesus Christ. This goal becomes our perspective, a sort of looking backward from there. Not much else matters if we have that end in sight. In the meantime, we must be grateful and responsible for our present surroundings without becoming so very attached that we lose sight of that goal of home. We hear terms such as *homesteader*, *homemaker*, *seeker*, and *pilgrim*. These describe those of us who, for scriptural reasons, see the dire necessity of separating from the current living standards in this country.

Home. For us it is a place of work, worthwhile work that has an extremely high level of productivity. With God's help, we are able to keep it full of fresh homegrown produce, our own milk, eggs, and meat. Homemade everything, from dresses to cereal to noodles. More importantly, it is our prayer that it will produce disciplined, contented people prepared to work for their heavenly Father—real home work.

Interview with Jerry Mander

Jerry Mander's importance to the debate over high technology cannot be overstated. * *Mary Ann and I visited him in San Francisco at the offices of Public Media Center, the country's only nonprofit advertising agency. We had planned to bring a shorthand stenographer to capture the interview, hoping to put this remarkable skill to good use, and also to avoid talking into a machine. But of course no stenographer or court reporter we contacted could forgo their PC to take up the pencil once again. That would be going backward!*

In the end, Public Media was able to supply a tape recorder. Our conversation was delayed, appropriately enough, as we tried to get the thing working. As it finally began to wind along, we ranged over topics that have gone on to form the sections of the rest of The Plain Reader: *health, work, media, community, and education.*

---

*He is the author of the first accessible critique of the modern mind-set on technology, *Four Arguments for the Elimination of Television* (New York: Morrow, 1978), as well as *In the Absence of the Sacred* (San Francisco: Sierra Club Books, 1991) and *The Case against the Global Economy*, coedited with Edward Goldsmith (San Francisco: Sierra Club Books, 1996).

An Interview with Jerry Mander

PLAIN MAGAZINE: You're working on free trade mostly right now, is that right? I don't want to call it *free trade*—you're working on globalization issues—can I put it that way?

JERRY MANDER: That's correct. Among other things, I'm working on a book, an anthology, together with Edward Goldsmith. He's the editor of the British publication *The Ecologist*. He's sort of the leading ecological battler in Europe over the last thirty years. He and I are compiling the book, titled *The Case against the Global Economy*. It's a very large anthology with about forty pieces in it.

The first part of the book is sort of a summary of all the dimensions concerning what is wrong about organizing life around global economic systems, from the point of view of how these systems break down nonwestern cultures, to the homogenization of existing western cultures, to corporate domination of economies, and the resulting detriment to communities and the destruction of small-scale farming.

PLAIN: I was going to say, a lot of food connections.

JM: Yes, one of the dimensions is globalization of the world food supply, with its serious effects on jobs, labor, and who has power over whom. And, of course, the many, many dire effects of this control on the Third World. Globalization destroys whatever sovereignty indigenous peoples have managed to gather up.

Also in the first part of the book is a small series of articles about what the consequences of globalization will be. Then the second part, "The Paradigms that Failed," discusses the operating paradigms by which the global economic system is motivating itself. These include continual economic growth, market economies, the idea of development, the idea of the supremacy of science, the idea of free trade.

The third part of the book is called "The Engines of Globalization" and has to do with the instruments by which globalization is taking its current form. Those instruments are mainly corporations and technology, and the way they interlock with one another.

Then the last section outlines the importance of returning to the local economy and strengthening that economy. Actually, maybe *Plain* should write something for that section!

PLAIN: I'm wondering about an idea that you have shared many times, something that you just touched on in describing *The Case against the Global Economy*—that institutional organization is itself a technological artifact of our time. It's an idea I have some trouble putting across to people. I wonder if you could say some more about it.

JM: The institution I talk about most is the corporation, and things like trade agreements, which are not so much expressions of technologies as they are in a symbiotic relationship to technologies, and to each other. Each makes the other one possible.

Corporations invent the technological forms, which then add power to the corporation, and then the corporation needs to create organizational structures in the world that will also aid the expanded operating possibilities made possible by technology. A computer is an example of a technology that makes globalization both possible and necessary.

In the modern world we have technologies of globalization. We have computers that tie the world together through cyberspace. People come to think of computers as empowering instruments, because they get to operate them and feed into them. And they are empowering in that narrow sense. But, those who are empowered the most by them are corporations, who can instantaneously move resources around the globe and control their megaform internationally, globally.

These transnational corporations are made stronger—they're actually made possible—by the new computer-laser-satellite technological linkups that enable them to move their resources and act globally in a manner they could not do as well nor as fast in the past.

PLAIN: So while we're all acting locally, and living locally, and, as Wendell Berry puts it (in a twist on the well-known slogan) "thinking locally," the larger corporations are . . .

JM: . . . Are acting globally and living globally and affecting globally. Actually, responding to the current situation by thinking locally and acting locally is, for me, a little bit insufficient. I think it's the right attitude to have, but at the same time you must be totally aware of the global, because it is acting on you all the time. You can do a lot of building up and protecting of things locally, and still see them wiped away anyway because of what is decided in world trade talks in Brussels.

In any case, these new technologies actually make the megacorporations possible on the global scale at which they now operate.

Other technologies of speed, like television and transportation, other forms of communication, space exploration—which enables resources on the globe to be photographed—all these things work together to speed up the development process to where global corporations conceive of themselves in global terms. But then they need to also have the ability to operate on global terms, without restrictions. The way this is achieved is by creating international structures that don't permit any local resistance.

By local, I don't mean your town or your community. I'm talking about the United States or any country's ability to exercise legal control over corporate activities, to the point that the United States, or any other country, can no longer make environmental laws, or consumer laws, or any kind of laws that protect people, or nature, or workers, or living conditions, or enact any restrictions that affect trade.

If it appears that there are restrictions on free corporate trade, then rules are made through instruments, such as trade agreements, that say, "All nations agree that they must not escape trade in the following ways. . . ." And they make lists of the ways each country may not restrain trade. If a country violates the rules, they can be challenged.

Europe will be able to challenge U.S. laws and the U.S. will be able to challenge Europe, and so by a reciprocal process back and forth, we void one another's laws. Then there will be no restrictions on corporate activity.

This is all instigated in some ways by advanced technological forms that themselves require operation on a global scale.

PLAIN: Technologies that require that they, too, be operated without any legal restraints, in order for them to work properly.

JM: Yes. It's really not a conscious conspiracy, in the way you would normally think of a conspiracy, as much as it is a conspiracy of forms. This is what I mean by its being technological, in the sense that once you have technologies like computers and satellites and all of those linkups that organize existence in a global manner, and you have corporations set up to use these technologies with great efficiency and ability, then you will have international political and economic systems that correspond to this globalized structure.

Or else you are going to have political and economic resistance to it. But resistance has already been wiped out by the operation of these forms.

PLAIN: The end of this process is rule by global corporations. In the long run, when most of the world has been culturally and economically supplanted—Americanized—if Borneo (to use an example) at some point decides not to cooperate, then it could be cut out of the loop. I mean, the people will have lost their ability to, say, grow their own food, and they'll be told, "Okay, if we can't have your forest for raw material, you can't have access anymore to the world food market."

JM: I wish that would happen. Because then you would have communities of people who are resisting. But these communities are being drawn into binding commitments not to resist. In fact, it is intolerable to the emerging global system that people be allowed to remain in their traditional cultural and economic spheres, because they are the market.

Bill Clinton says we need to expand our markets, and the reason we need to expand our markets is that we have pretty much used up the United States as a market. You know, people are up to their necks in consumption.

PLAIN: Everybody has a lot of stuff.

JM: And there is only so much stuff you can have, actually, even though consumer goods are always being updated so that people will need to purchase the new—computers, for example. But still, there is just a diminishing return on this market, and so you need to have China as a market, you need to have Indonesia as a market, you need to have India as a market. And in order to have them as markets, they have to want to be like us.

PLAIN: They have to want what we're selling.

JM: And television is how this is achieved. Television is the ideological invasion. The exposure to western culture through television creates in other cultures the desire to be like us and to buy our products.

PLAIN: Television is pretty powerful. It works. It has worked quite well here in the U.S. However, I see an ongoing process whereby Americans are becoming surfeited with consumption. I suppose that by the time we are ready as a society to turn away from consumerism, we will have hooked the rest of the world on it.

JM: The idea of globalization is to replace these consumers with other consumers. What is going to happen when U.S. corporations—which are already engaged in relocating outside the U.S.—begin moving even more rapidly out of this country to other, low-wage countries? When all production is moved to Mexico?

PLAIN: That's no problem. After all, we're an information economy now. We don't need to have production here. We are just the guys who, for example, figure out the flight schedules to move a banana harvest halfway around the world, so that people can buy bananas year-round instead of growing and preserving their own fruits. We're the service sector, the middleman. We don't need to actually produce anything here in the United States. Or so we're told.

JM: Jeremy Rifkin notes in his book *The End of Work* that the number of real jobs in the United States is shrinking. Everyone is being replaced by robots. Not only in manufacturing; automation is occurring in all sectors, including the information sector.

PLAIN: They're next. They just don't know it yet.

JM: The service sector is where the new jobs are supposed to be. The industrial sector is finished, because it's all robots. The agricultural sector is being replaced by biotechnologies and automated factory farms. And it is claimed that these losses do not matter because we still have the service sector, the information economy. But you go to the library . . . and there are no librarians! You go to the bank and there are no bankers! Go to McDonald's and there's hardly anyone working there. Most of the work is being done by machines.

PLAIN: And those workers who have been replaced—those are all layoffs.

JM: Which brings us to the question of what constitutes efficiency. Wherever you see it reported in a newspaper that, for example, General Motors has improved its efficiency, what is meant is that they have replaced their workers, and replaced them with machines. They have downsized their workforce in order to improve efficiency.

PLAIN: This is similar to what has already occurred in agriculture, where modern agriculture has replaced people and communities with technologies based on ready access to cheap energy. The emerging global economy seems based on the same idea that we can just cart things all over the world. That you can sit in your home and video-shop, and somewhere in Indonesia a robot will produce the requested item, which will be delivered to your door the next day.

JM: However, as Jeremy Rifkin points out, as automation increases and corporations move out of the country, the market in the United States will begin to diminish, because people won't be able to buy things. So there will be a deflated market potential in this country. Which brings us back to the importance of building markets in other countries. People in these countries have to be given some buying power; but they are being paid such low wages that they won't individually have much buying power, anyway. There is a climax coming, where these two contradictory conditions will come together.

PLAIN: And of course that's where it all started. At the beginning of the age of mass production and the mass economy, with Henry Ford saying he wanted to pay his workers enough so they could buy his car.

JM: That's right.

PLAIN: As people who intentionally live apart from modernity, what we call being separated from "the world," we're frequently asked if our way of life doesn't limit us, narrow our perspective, or make us less open-minded in some way. For example, we sometimes have to remind those who think we don't know what is going on in the world (since we don't have TVs or radios), that we can always pick up a newspaper if it seems worthwhile to do so. What's your experience with the level of consciousness of those who embrace modernity?

JM: I think of people living in the technological framework as perhaps very limited and narrowed, in comparison with those who live outside it, because the technological framework is a knowledge system that is extremely channeled compared to other forms of knowing.

I just came back from having lunch with my friend Jeannette Armstrong. She speaks of native ways of knowledge—native "knowing"—and indigenous systems of communication. She has written an essay for *The Case against the Global Economy* entitled "Sharing One Skin," about her people's idea of community, where the community lives as an extended family, one that also includes the role of ancestors and the role of the future projection of the community.

PLAIN: So it's four-dimensional.

JM: It's actually six-dimensional, because it has the four physical directions, but then it has the past and future also, so it is a very comprehensive way of experiencing one's self and community in the world.

And that's all wiped out by something like television, for example, which brings you only the now, and which is very forcefully one-dimensional.

PLAIN: And it's all up in the head. We could call this the culture of the disembodied brain. That's what we seem to be working on. . . .

I wonder, however, if we say that people will be totally altered by this one-dimensionality, if we assume they won't even notice they're living like machines. I'm not at all pessimistic because I know we each have something inside us capable of resisting such evil.

JM: In every generation there is a spectrum of reactions to the dominant paradigm. So you and I have reacted in a particular way to what we've been presented with, and so we, along with some others, may be expressions of the kind of resistance to domination that you're describing. That's the hope—that many people do see it and will resist it. And I do think resistance is growing in the U.S.

But the opposite is also true, I'm sorry to say. The point of these technologies is to create people of a certain kind to populate the dominant society, and that is occurring. People who use a heavy amount of television are experiencing . . . television! As their life. People who use computers a large part of their day are not experiencing higher consciousness the way they think they are; they're experiencing computers. By the mode of interaction that modern technologies impose, users slowly evolve into people who relate to these instruments and have adjusted to them. So I do think it changes the human being, and this is the reason for speaking about it and resisting it and challenging it as much as we possibly can.

If you were right and everyone has the ability to resist this . . . I think some people have the ability to resist, because they're just lucky or have trained themselves to think systematically about technology. But many people (for whatever reason, and without being critical of them, I just think it's a fact) many people do not question technologies as they are introduced, and do absorb them and do turn into a kind of machine person, serving the larger machine to a much greater extent than in prior times. That is a tragedy, and what we need to organize against and speak about. It's the reason you have a magazine such as *Plain*.

PLAIN: In a way. But we are not saying that everyone has inside of them the concrete means—the tools—to resist. Our perspective would be that what everyone has inside of them is God. Everyone is endowed with a soul, which is a part of God and allows them to commune with God.

I've been running an experiment for the last three years, which is I talk to just about everyone about these issues—anybody. I talk to people who are just as you've described, but I have never had anyone say to me, "No, no, get away from me. These issues aren't important to me. I like being a machine." On the contrary, in every case where I've spoken heart-to-heart about my concerns, they've turned around and said, "You know, I, too, have a real sense of unease about what I'm doing. I think I do watch too much television. I do feel controlled by it," etc. Now, if I were to wag my finger at them, or organize activities to "wake them up," appealing to their minds, they would simply hold more tightly to their stake in the dominant culture. When I tell them my fears and failings, I've not had a single person fail to respond. And so I do believe this is how we're going to reach people. Our magazine reaches people by dissolving their fear, by encouraging others with what we're doing.

JM: I agree, and I was responding to your comment that perhaps this system can't succeed in creating these dominant forms, because I think it can succeed, and has succeeded. I also do think that everyone has a seed of awareness, and given the opportunity they will respond to that. And the response can be stimulated and fed. It is also true that many people are so engulfed and so surrounded by a singular reality, that they don't get touched by that. It's like being immersed in an isolation tank. They don't know what's outside it. I use the example of "the madness of the astronaut," as I call it. Separated from earth, in a metallic reality, all systems provided from some other place, no connection to source, whirling around without roots, strictly a world of mind, living in a completely homocentric artificial reality without any sense of connection to anything. It's very hard for that person to maintain contact with reality.

PLAIN: How vulnerable that person is.

JM: Oh, incredibly vulnerable! People caught up in that situation have nowhere to turn. I think you can make the case that this society is increasingly telling people to live that way. In Epcot Centers, in Disney Worlds. San Francisco is a nice city compared to most, but there's no nature around here anywhere you look. Living or working here, it's very hard to remember that there is something that came before this, that there's something underneath it.

PLAIN: This brings us then to the question of tactics. If everyone is carrying a potential awareness of the wrongness of modern life—a human or spiritual nature is in there that is aware it is being abused on some level—my experience tells me that traditional activism (appealing to our moral outrage or sense of fairness, or just providing the information we've been blocked from receiving), that approach probably isn't going to activate their higher nature.

JM: Sometimes it can. It sometimes confirms what they might already feel, or shows them a community of people who feel as they do.

PLAIN: That is a key then. Do we feel that others also have concerns about modern life. Do we feel there is hope.

There is an essay in *Plain* by Wendell Berry ["Health Is Membership," page 49] in which he talks about the power of love, which in its divine form he sees as the organizing power of the universe. And he suggests that we need to tap into this source when we are confronted with the massive and apparently invincible technological superstructure. That's how we're going to get somewhere—not so much through agitation and activism but by going to the person who is trapped in the system and telling them you know they're trapped. And that you have been trapped, too. And that will get through to them.

JM: The important thing is for people to be very conscious of their actions in the world, very conscious of what is being acted on them, and then devote time to separating from the harmful while still staying in touch enough to affect what's going on.

PLAIN [Mary Ann]: Earlier today we had lunch with the editors of a high-technology magazine, and the operations chief asked me a question, "Scott made a choice to live the way your family is living now, and I assume you did, too—you weren't brought up this

way—but what about your children? You're raising them in isolation from what constitutes normal life for most children. Are they going to be able to make a choice when they're older?"

Now, this person who asked me happens to have an infant son, so I asked him in return, "Well, is your child going to be able to make a choice?"

[Scott]: And his answer was very telling, really. Everybody at the table laughed, because Mary Ann had turned the question back to him, but then he said something like, "Well, I'm hoping he will go to college and get a good liberal arts education."

[Mary Ann]: He said his child would be educated in institutions.

[Scott]: And when he finished, everyone laughed again, good-naturedly, of course, but because they could see the absurdity. He was thinking that because our children are not exposed to modern technology and consumer culture, they won't have the information needed to make a choice later on about how to live. When in reality, raising children in the dominant culture is much more likely to "lock in" their future lives. Anyone can learn to use a computer after they have grown up.

[Mary Ann]: One of the things we're trying to convey through the magazine is letting people know that they can make choices about how to live. The person who questioned me today believed that in order for my children to make choices when they are teenagers or adults, I cannot make any choices right now. I have to follow the worldly culture.

JM: It appears he doesn't recognize that the culture he's in is already a rigid system of preset choices and channels and paradigms and assumptions. That is a far more limiting culture.

PLAIN [Scott]: Let's talk about computers and children. Our experience has been that people readily accept putting the two together without any reservations. It's just a given that somehow your children will be better educated.

[Mary Ann]: From what I've seen, people are really pushing it. The premise is that if your three-year-old doesn't start getting familiar with computers, he or she is going to be lost.

JM: They'll just be left behind!

PLAIN: But that doesn't make sense on the face of it, because there are thousands or millions of people making their livings with very sophisticated computer systems, who didn't have them when they were three years old!

My concern is that while children at such a young age are doing computers—because parents believe they won't be able to catch up later—they aren't spending time doing all sorts of other things I know they can't catch up on later in life. Oh, they may be able to color and cut and paste when they're twenty, but that's not when their developing bodies and minds need to do that. In any event, they are being deprived of time needed to do the traditional things we associate with the healthy development of children.

JM: I'm not an expert on the topic of children and computers, although I have some opinions about them. The expert to speak to is Chet Bowers from Portland State University. I've learned a lot from him. What he says about computers in education is that they are actually dangerous if you are interested in having your child maintain an ecological world view and maintain fully operative knowledge systems and communication systems.

The way he explains it, computers train the mind in a certain way. By operating computers, children are learning a certain way of thinking, a certain way of knowing. They're dealing with an information field that is digital as opposed to multisensory and that is training the mind to think within a certain kind of system, bringing information only of the kind that is translatable through a machine— aside from the fact that they are experiencing their day relating to a machine and getting their knowledge from a machine and in the narrow forms that a machine can deliver.

The effect of that is to amplify these ways of thinking and experiencing. Learning of a digital nature. It's been said that data is being substituted for knowledge and wisdom. And you're getting a simultaneous suppression of the previous forms of knowing. The net effect is that you are creating human beings who are attuned to the modern machine consciousness and machine world, human beings that therefore probably will function better in that milieu than your children will.

PLAIN: Jane Healy in her book *Endangered Minds* goes so far as to say that possibly brain structure of future generations is going to be changed.

JM: A lot of people are saying that.

PLAIN: Because, at an age when children's brains are still growing, different neuronal pathways are being laid down from what one might expect in a child who is raised without television or computers.

JM: Joseph Chilton Pierce says, and I believe he's right, that no child—even if the parents are not flat-out against television—no child under the age of eleven should watch television.

PLAIN: That's pretty much the Waldorf Education view.

JM: My criticism of computers is not so much about children, it's a much broader critique. I do a systemic critique of computers. My problem with them is that they've come along riding this wave of glorious utopian vision, and that everyone is looking at the upside of them. Even the people who are supposed to be smart and critical, like those high-technology magazine editors you met with today, are so excited about the empowerment they feel from being able to zap their E-mail around to communicate with their like-minded partners, that they have never bothered to do any practical or informed systemic analysis.

That's often the case with modern technologies. We don't have a critical attitude, so we have no way to evaluate them. For me, when you apply a systemic analysis to computers, you find out that this so-called empowerment you get from computers is minuscule compared to the empowerment that global corporations and centralized systems get.

Computers can be also [environmentally and physically] toxic. They change the way we think and the way we know. They separate people from community. They create virtual community, which is not community. They confuse people as to what is community, what is reality. They objectify information in such a way that you can no longer get a real sense of the natural world. They are training people to understand nature only in the terms by which computers can describe it.

The most important part of a systemic critique would be to

understand what computers make possible with other technologies. In other words, computers are the base for another generation of new technologies that are even more frightening.

PLAIN: Genetic engineering.

JM: Yes, and robotics, space exploration, nanotechnologies. . . . All kinds of very bizarre and horrible technologies could not exist without computers. Computers are the window by which those other systems can be introduced. So, obviously computers are bringing with them a brand-new world of technological takeover that couldn't possibly exist without them. That is also part of a systemic critique of computers.

In a truly democratic society, we would say, "Let's have a debate about this. Let's understand all the future consequences of this technology before we embrace it." But in this society, we just embrace it.

There's no thinking about the consequences, and if I start listing them, people think I'm odd, or they question why I am being so "negative" instead of telling about the glorious unification that could happen through computers. Well, what's happening is that there is unification taking place, but it is the corporations and the global economy that are becoming more unified than we are.

PLAIN: To me that's the crucial point of a systemic critique. The activist environmentalists say, "Isn't it great, I can use this computer to fight the clear-cutting of the forests by global corporations." But the reason the forests are being cut down with such alacrity is because the global corporations have computers. So, we should be asking ourselves how we can contribute to the end of computers.

JM: In essence, we'd be better off without the technology. The fundamental questions you have to ask are, "Do we need it? If we need it, what do we need it for?" In other words, on what grounds do we think this technology is a good thing? That whole process of making a decision is not a part of our culture, yet.

My critique is along these lines. How computers affect children is just one of many points. Computers in schools serve as an example of our inability to critique this technology. Computers in schools—this technology is taking over everything! Computerization of schools is advancing by leaps and bounds. Corporations are free to put computers in all the schools, in order to train kids in how to use them. Apple Computer is one of the most guilty in this process. Kids are learning how to process all information through computers, and teachers are being eliminated as the technology replaces them. And there has been no discussion of it in the schools.

PLAIN: No, none.

JM: No discussion! No discussion! No questioning, Is this a good idea or a bad idea?

PLAIN: Well . . . no discussion needed. It's a good idea, period. No discussion needed, or allowed.

ON THE EARTH...

. . . IN THE TECHNOSPHERE

Choosing Health

If there had never been an Industrial Revolution, we would have a very different notion of what health care is. Would the care of our health be better or worse without the technology and organizational structures that characterize modern medicine? I have personally encountered such deep discrepancies between the claims of medicine and what it delivers that I can't help wondering. Alternatives to establishment medicine that have worked for our family—herbal and natural remedies, good nutrition, manipulative therapies, home birth— are all really elaborated extensions of the "folk" medicine that predated modern life. These forms of health care represent the directions our culture was taking prior to the turn toward a medical model based on technology and the elevation of treating illness over the encouragement of wellness.

If there had never been an Industrial Revolution, and all of our healing impulses and productivity had gone into perfecting the technologies of wellness, we might have arrived at a sense of health that is many times more humane than that of the medical model. We might by now have learned to integrate our ministrations into life's powerful natural passages of birth, growth, aging, and death.

Fortunately, the plain people have never lost the folk sense that so many of us crave and are rediscovering (including—belatedly—the medical researchers, if not the actual practitioners). The best of this folk sense is exemplified by the understanding that mind, body, and spirit exist in a continuum, are connected, are parts in a whole. Wendell Berry perceives this same truth and articulates it when he says that "Health is membership."

Health Is Membership

WENDELL BERRY

From our constant and increasing concerns about health, you can tell how seriously diseased we are. Health, as we may remember from at least some of the days of our youth, is at once wholeness and a kind of unconsciousness. Disease (dis-ease), on the contrary, makes us conscious not only of the state of our health, but of the division of our bodies and our world into parts.

The word "health," in fact, comes from the same Indo-European root as "heal," "whole," and "holy." To be healthy is literally to be whole; to heal is to make whole. I don't think mortal healers should be credited with the power to make holy. But I have no doubt that such healers are properly obliged to acknowledge and respect the holiness embodied in all creatures, or that our healing involves the preservation in us of the spirit and the breath of God.

If we were lucky enough as children to be surrounded by grownups who loved us, then our sense of wholeness is not just the sense of completeness-in-ourselves, but is the sense also of belonging to others and to our place; it is an unconscious awareness of community, of having-in-common. It may be that this double sense of singular integrity and of communal belonging is our personal standard of health for as long as we live. Anyhow, we seem to know instinctively that health is not divided.

Of course, growing up and growing older as fallen creatures in a

49

fallen world can only instruct us painfully in division and disintegration. This is the stuff of consciousness and experience. But if our culture works in us as it should, we do not age merely into disintegration and division, but that very experience begins our education, leading us into knowledge of wholeness and of holiness. I am describing here the story of Job, of Lazarus, of the lame man at the pool of Bethesda, of Milton's Samson, of King Lear. If our culture works in us as it should, our experience is balanced by education; we are led out of our lonely suffering and are made whole.

In the present age of the world, disintegration and division, isolation and suffering seem to have overwhelmed us. The balance between experience and education has been overthrown; we are lost in experience, and so-called education is leading us nowhere. We have diseases aplenty. As if that were not enough, we are suffering an almost universal hypochondria. Half the energy of the medical industry, one suspects, may now be devoted to "examinations"—to see if, though apparently well, we may not be latently or insidiously diseased.

If you are going to deal with the issue of health in the modern world, you are going to have to deal with much absurdity. It is not clear, for example, why death should increasingly be looked upon as a curable disease, an abnormality, by a society that increasingly looks upon life as insupportably painful and/or meaningless. Even more startling is the realization that the modern medical industry faithfully imitates disease in the way that it isolates us and parcels us out. If, for example, intense and persistent pain causes you to pay attention only to your stomach, then you must leave home, community, and family, and go to a sometimes distant clinic or hospital, where you will be cared for by a specialist who will pay attention only to your stomach.

Or consider the announcement by the Associated Press on February 9, 1994, that "the incidence of cancer is up among all ages, and researchers speculated that environmental exposure to cancer-causing substances other than cigarettes may be partly to blame." This bit of news is offered as a surprise, never mind that the environment (so-called) has been known to be polluted and toxic for many years. The blame obviously falls on that idiotic term "the environment," which refers to a world that surrounds us but is presumably different from us and distant from us. Our laboratories have proved long ago that cigarette smoke gets inside us, but if "the environment" surrounds us, how does it wind up inside us? So much for division as a working principle of health.

This, plainly, is a view of health that is severely reductive. It is, to begin with, almost fanatically individualistic. The body is seen as a defective or potentially defective machine, singular, solitary, and displaced, without love, solace, or pleasure. Its health excludes unhealthy cigarettes, but does not exclude unhealthy food, water, and air. One may presumably be healthy in a disintegrated family or community, or in a destroyed or poisoned ecosystem.

So far, I have been implying my beliefs at every turn. Now I had better state them openly.

I take literally the statement in the Gospel of John that God loves the world. I believe that the world was created and approved by love, that it subsists, coheres, and endures by love, and that, insofar as it is redeemable, it can be redeemed only by love. I believe that divine love, incarnate and indwelling in the world, summons the world always toward wholeness, which is ultimately reconciliation and atonement with God.

I believe that health is wholeness. For many years I have returned again and again to the work of the English agriculturalist, Sir Albert Howard, who said, in *The Soil and Health*, that "the whole problem of health in soil, plant, animal, and man [is] one great subject."

I am moreover a Luddite, in what I take to be the true and

appropriate sense. I am not "against technology" so much as I am for community. When the choice is between the health of a community and technological innovation, I choose the health of the community. I would unhesitatingly destroy a machine before I would allow the machine to destroy my community.

I believe that the community—in the fullest sense, a place and all its creatures—is the smallest unit of health, and that to speak of the health of an isolated individual is a contradiction in terms.

We speak now of "spirituality and healing" as if the only way to render a proper religious respect to the body is somehow to treat it "spiritually." It could be argued just as appropriately (and perhaps less dangerously) that the way to respect the body fully is to honor fully its materiality. In saying this, I intend no reduction. I do not doubt the reality of the experience and knowledge we call "spiritual" any more than I doubt the reality of so-called "physical" experience and knowledge; I recognize the rough utility of these terms. But I strongly doubt the advantage, and even the possibility, of separating these two realities.

What I'm laboring against here is not complexity or mystery, but what I take to be an absurd and destructive dualism. I would like to purge my own mind and language of such terms as "spiritual," "physical," "metaphysical," and "transcendental"—all of which imply that the Creation is divided by fault lines into "levels" that can readily be peeled apart and judged by human beings. I believe that the Creation is one continuous fabric comprehending simultaneously what we mean by "spirit" and what we mean by "matter."

Our bodies are involved in the world. Their needs and desires and pleasures are physical. Our bodies hunger and thirst, yearn toward other bodies, grow tired and seek rest, rise up rested, eager to exert themselves. All these desires may be satisfied with honor to the body and its Maker, but only if much else besides the individual body is brought into consideration. We have long known that individual desires must not be made the standard of their own satisfaction. We must consider the body's manifold connections to other bodies and to the world. The body, "fearfully and wonderfully made," is ultimately mysterious both in itself and in its dependences. Our bodies live, the Bible says, by the spirit and the breath of God, but it does not say how this is so. We are not going to *know* about this.

The distinction between the physical and the spiritual is, I believe, false. A much more valid distinction, and the one that we need urgently to learn to make, is that between the organic and the mechanical. To argue this—as I am going to do—puts me in the minority, I know, but it does not make me unique. In *The Idea of a Christian Society*, T. S. Eliot wrote: "We may say that religion, as distinguished from modern paganism, implies a life in conformity with nature. It may be observed that the natural life and the supernatural life have a conformity to each other which neither has with the mechanistic life. . . ."

Still, I wonder if our sometimes wish to deal spiritually with physical things does not come either from the feeling that physical things are "low" and unworthy, or from the fear, especially when speaking of affection, that "physical" will be taken to mean "sexual."

The *New York Review of Books* of February 3, 1994, for example, carried a review of the correspondence of William and Henry James along with a photograph of the two brothers standing together, with William's arm around Henry's shoulders. Apropos of this picture, the reviewer, John Bayley, wrote that "their closeness of affection was undoubted and even took on occasion a quasi-physical form." It is Mr. Bayley's qualifier *quasi-physical* that sticks in one's mind. What can he have meant by it? Is this prurience masquerading as squeamishness, or vice versa? Does Mr. Bayley feel a need to alert his psychologically sophisticated readers to the possibility that, even though these brothers touched one another familiarly, they were not homosexual lovers?

The phrase involves at least some version of the old dualism of spirit and body or mind and body that has caused us so much suffering and trouble, and that raises such troubling questions for anybody who is interested in health. If you love your brother, and if you and your brother are living creatures, how could your love for him not be physical? Not spiritual or mental only, not "quasi-physical," but physical. How could you not take a simple pleasure in putting your arm around him?

Out of the same dualism comes our confusion about the body's proper involvement in the world. People seriously interested in health will finally have to question our society's long-standing goals of convenience and effortlessness. What is the point of "labor-saving" if by making work effortless we make it poor, and if by doing poor work we weaken our bodies and lose conviviality and health?

We are now pretty clearly involved in a crisis of health, one of the wonders of which is its immense profitability, both to those who cause it and to those who propose to cure it. That the illness may prove incurable, except by catastrophe, is suggested by our economic dependence on it. Think, for example, of how readily our solutions become problems and our cures pollutants. To cure one disease, we need another. The causes, of course, are numerous and complicated, but all of them, I think, can be traced back to the old idea that our bodies are not very important except when they give us pleasure (usually, now, to somebody's profit) or when they hurt (now, almost invariably, to somebody's profit).

This dualism inevitably reduces physical reality, and it does so by removing its mystery from it, by dividing it absolutely from what dualistic thinkers have understood as spiritual or mental reality.

A reduction that is merely theoretical might be harmless enough, I suppose, but theories find ways of getting into action. The theory of the relative unimportance of physical reality has put itself into action by means of a metaphor by which the body (along with the world itself) is understood as a machine. According to this metaphor—which is now in constant general use—the human heart, for example, is no longer understood as the center of our emotional life or even as an organ that pumps; it is understood as "a pump," having somewhat the same functions as a fuel pump in an automobile.

If the body is a machine for living and working, then it must follow that the mind is a machine for thinking. The "progress" here is the reduction of mind to brain and then of brain to computer. This reduction implies and requires the reduction of knowledge to "information." It requires, in fact, the reduction of everything to numbers and mathematical operations.

This metaphor of the machine bears heavily upon the question of what we mean by health and by healing. The problem is that, like any metaphor, it is accurate only in some respects. A girl is only in some respects like a red rose; a heart is only in some respects like a pump. This means that a metaphor must be controlled by a sort of humorous intelligence, always mindful of the exact limits within which the comparison is meaningful. When a metaphor begins to control intelligence, as this one of the machine has done for a long time, then we must look for costly distortions and absurdities.

Of course, the body in most ways is not at all like a machine. Like all living creatures, and unlike a machine, the body is not formally self-contained; its boundaries and outlines are not so exactly fixed. The body alone is not, properly speaking, a body. Divided from its sources of air, food, drink, clothing, shelter, and companionship, a body is, properly speaking, a cadaver; whereas a machine by itself, shut down or out of fuel, is still a machine. Merely as an organism (leaving aside issues of mind and spirit) the body lives and moves and has its being, minute by minute, by an interinvolvement with other bodies and other creatures, living and unliving, that is too complex to diagram or describe. It is, moreover, under the influence of thought and feeling. It does not live by "fuel" alone.

A mind, probably, is even less like a computer than a body is like a machine. As far as I am able to understand it, a mind is not even much like a brain. Insofar as it is usable for thought, for the association of thought with feeling, for the association of thoughts and feelings with words, for the connections between words and things, words and acts, thought and memory, a mind seems to be in constant need of reminding. A mind unreminded would be no mind at all. This phenomenon of reminding shows the extensiveness of mind—how intricately it is involved with sensation, emotion, memory, tradition, communal life, known landscapes, and so on. How could you locate a mind within its full extent, among all its subjects and necessities, I don't know, but obviously it cannot be located within a brain or a computer.

To see better what a mind is (or is not) it is useful to consider the difference between what we mean by knowledge and what the computer now requires us to mean by "information." Knowledge refers to the ability to do or say the right thing at the right time; we could not speak of somebody who does the wrong thing at the wrong time as "knowledgeable." People who perform well as musicians, athletes, teachers, or farmers are people of knowledge. And such examples tell us much about the nature of knowledge. Knowledge is formal, and it informs speech and action. It is instantaneous; it is present and available when and where it is needed.

"Information," which once meant that which forms or fashions from within, now means merely *data*. However organized this data may be, it is not shapely or formal or in the true sense in-forming. It is not present where it is needed; if you have to "access" it, you don't have it. Whereas knowledge moves and forms acts, "information" is inert. You cannot imagine a debater or a quarterback or a musician performing by "accessing information." A computer chock full of such information is no more admirable than a head or a book chock full of it.

The difference, then, between information and knowledge is something like the difference between a dictionary and somebody's language.

Where the art and science of healing are concerned, the machine metaphor works to enforce a division that falsifies the process of healing because it falsifies the nature of the creature needing to be healed. If the body is a machine, then its diseases can be healed by a sort of mechanical tinkering, without reference to anything outside the body itself. This applies, with obvious differences, to the mind; people are assumed to be individually sane or insane. And so we return to the utter anomaly of a creature who is healthy within itself.

The modern hospital, where most of us receive our strictest lessons in the nature of industrial medicine, undoubtedly does well at surgery and other procedures that permit the body and its parts to be treated as separate things. But when you try to think of it as a place of healing—of reconnecting and making whole—then the hospital becomes a revelation of the disarray of the medical industry's thinking about health.

In healing, the body is restored to itself. It begins to live again by its own powers and instincts, to the extent that it can do so. To the extent that it can do so, it goes free of drugs and mechanical helps. Its appetites return. It relishes food and rest. The patient is restored to family and friends, home and community and work.

This process has a certain naturalness and inevitability, like that by which a child grows up, but industrial medicine seems to grasp it only tentatively and awkwardly. For example, any ordinary person would assume that a place of healing would put a premium upon rest, but hospitals are notoriously difficult to sleep in. They are noisy all night, and the routine interventions go on relentlessly. The body is treated as a machine that does not need to rest.

You would think also that a place dedicated to healing and health would make much of food. But here is where the disconnections of the industrial system and the displacement of industrial humanity are most radical. Sir Albert Howard saw accurately that the issue of human health is inseparable from the health of the soil, and he saw, too, that we humans must responsibly occupy our place in the cycle of birth, growth, maturity, death, and decay that is the health of the world. Aside from our own mortal involvement, food is our fundamental connection to that cycle. But probably most of the complaints you hear about hospitals have to do with the food, which, according to the testimony I have heard, tends to range from unappetizing to sickening. Food is treated as another unpleasant substance to inject. And this is a shame. For in addition to the obvious nutritional link between food and health, food can be a pleasure. People who are sick are often troubled or depressed, and mealtimes offer three opportunities a day when patients could easily be offered something to look forward to. Nothing is more pleasing or heartening than a plate of nourishing, tasty, beautiful food artfully and lovingly prepared. Anything less is unhealthy and also a desecration of all that is involved.

Why should rest and food and ecological health not be the basic principles of our art and science of healing? Is it because the basic principles already are technology and drugs? Are we confronting some fundamental incompatibility between mechanical efficiency and organic health? I don't know. I only know that sleeping in a hospital is like sleeping in a factory, and that the medical industry makes only the most tenuous connection between health and food and no connection between health and the soil. Industrial medicine is as little interested in ecological health as is industrial agriculture.

A further problem, and an equally serious one, is that illness, in addition to being a bodily disaster, is now also an economic disaster. This is so, whether or not the patient is insured. It is a disaster for us all, all the time, because we all know that, personally or collectively, we cannot continue to pay for cures that continue to get more expensive. The economic disturbance that now inundates the problem of illness may turn out to be the profoundest illness of all. How can we get well if we are worried sick about money?

I wish it were not the fate of this essay to be surrounded by questions, but questions now seem the inescapable end of any line of thought about health and healing. Here are several more:

1. Can our present medical industry produce an adequate definition of health? My own guess is that it cannot do so. Like industrial agriculture, industrial medicine has depended increasingly on specialist methodology, mechanical technology, and chemicals, and so its point of reference has become more and more its own technical prowess and less and less the health of creatures and habitats. I don't expect this problem to be solved in the universities, which have never addressed, much less solved, the problem of health in agriculture. And I don't expect it to be solved by the government.

2. How can cheapness be included in the criteria of medical experimentation and performance? And why has it not been included before now? I believe that the problem here is again that of the medical industry's fixation on specialization, technology, and chemistry. The modern "health care system" thus has become a way of marketing industrial products, exactly like modern agriculture, impoverishing those who pay and enriching those who are paid. It is, in other words, an industry, such as industries have always been.

3. Why is it that medical strictures and recommendations so often work in favor of food processors, and against food producers? Why, for example, do we so strongly favor the pasteurization of

milk to health and cleanliness in milk production? (Gene Logsdon correctly says that the motive here "is monopoly, not consumer health.")

4. Why do we so strongly prefer a fat-free or a germ-free diet to a chemical-free diet? Why does the medical industry, which strenuously opposes the use of tobacco, complacently and passively accept the massive use of antibiotics and other drugs in meat animals and of poisons on food crops? How much longer can it cling to the superstition of bodily health in a polluted world?

5. How can adequate medical and health care, including disease prevention, be included in the structure and economy of a community? How, for example, can a community and its doctors be included in the same culture, the same knowledge, and the same fate, so that they will live as fellow citizens, sharers in a common wealth, members of one another?

It is clear by now that this essay cannot hope to be complete; the problems are too large and my knowledge too small. What I have to offer is an association of thoughts and questions wandering somewhat at random and somewhat lost within the experience of modern diseases and the often bewildering industry that undertakes to cure them. In my ignorance and bewilderment, I am fairly representative of those who go, or go with loved ones, to doctors' offices and hospitals. What I have written so far comes from my various efforts to make as much sense as I can of that experience. But now I had better turn to the experience itself.

On January 3, 1994, my brother, John, had a severe heart attack while he was out by himself on his farm, moving a feed trough. He managed to get to the house and telephone a friend, who sent the emergency rescue squad.

The rescue squad and the emergency room staff at a local hospital certainly saved my brother's life. He was later moved to a hospital in Louisville, where a surgeon performed a "double bypass" operation on his heart. After three weeks John returned home. He still has a life to live and work to do. He has been restored to himself and to the world.

He and those who love him have a considerable debt to the medical industry, as represented by two hospitals, several doctors and nurses, many drugs, and many machines. This is a debt that I cheerfully acknowledge. But I am obliged to say also that my experience of the hospital during John's stay was troubled by much conflict of feeling and a good many unresolved questions, and I know that I am not alone in this.

In the hospital what I will call the world of love meets the world of efficiency—the world, that is, of specialization, machinery, and abstract procedure. Or, rather, I should say that these two worlds come together in the hospital, but do not meet. During those weeks in the hospital, it seemed to me that my brother had come from the world of love, and that the family members, neighbors, and friends who at various times were there with him came there to represent that world and to preserve his connection with it. It seemed to me that the hospital was another kind of world altogether.

When I said earlier that we live in a world that was created and exists and is redeemable by love, I did not mean to sentimentalize it. For this also is a fallen world. It involves error and disease, ignorance and partiality, sin and death. If this world is a place where we may learn of our involvement in immortal love, as I believe it is, still such learning is possible here because that love involves us so inescapably in the limits, suffering, and sorrows of mortality.

Like divine love, earthly love seeks plentitude; it longs for all the members to be joined. Unlike divine love, earthly love does not have the power, the knowledge, or the will to achieve what it longs for. The story of human love on this earth is a story by which this love reveals and even validates itself by its failures to be complete or comprehensive enough or effective enough. When this love enters a hospital, it brings with it a terrifying history of defeat, but it comes nevertheless confident of itself, for its existence and the power of its longing have been proved over and over again even by its defeat. In the face of illness, the threat of death, and death itself, it insists unabashedly on its own presence, understanding by its persistence through defeat that it is superior to whatever happens.

The world of efficiency ignores both loves, earthly and divine, because by definition it must reduce experience to computation, particularly to abstraction, mystery to a small comprehensibility. Efficiency, in our present sense of the word, allies itself inevitably with machinery, as Neil Postman demonstrates in his useful book *Technopoly*. "Machines," he says, "eliminate complexity, doubt, and ambiguity. They work swiftly, they are standardized, and they provide us with numbers that you can see and calculate with." To reason, the advantages are obvious, and probably no reasonable person would wish to reject them out of hand.

And yet love obstinately answers that no loved one is standardized. A body, love insists, is neither a spirit nor a machine; it is not a picture, a diagram, a chart, a graph, an anatomy; it is not an explanation; it is not a law. It is precisely and uniquely what it is. It belongs to the world of love, which is a world of living creatures, natural orders and cycles, many small, fragile lights in the dark.

I had thought much, in dealing with problems of agriculture, of the difference between creatures and machines. But I never so clearly understood and felt that difference as when John was in recovery after his heart surgery, when he was attached to many machines and was dependent for breath on a respirator. It was impossible then not to see that the breathing of a machine, like all machine work, is unvarying, an oblivious regularity, whereas the breathing of a creature is ever changing, exquisitely responsive to events both inside and outside the body, to thoughts and emotions.

A machine makes breaths as a machine makes buttons, all the same, but every breath of a creature is itself a creature, like no other, inestimably precious.

Logically, in plentitude some things ought to be expendable. Industrial economics has always believed this: Abundance justifies waste. This is one of the dominant superstitions of American history—and of the history of colonialism everywhere. Expendability is also an assumption of the world of efficiency, which is why that world deals so compulsively in percentages of efficacy, or safety, or whatever.

But this sort of logic is absolutely alien to the world of love. To the claim that a certain drug or procedure would save 99 percent of all cancer patients or that a certain pollutant would be safe for 99 percent of a population, love, unembarrassed, would respond, "What about the 1 percent?"

There is nothing rational or perhaps even defensible about this, but it is nonetheless one of the strongest strands of our religious tradition—it is probably the most essential strand—according to which a shepherd, owning a hundred sheep and having lost one, does not say, "I have saved 99 percent of my sheep," but rather, "I have lost one," and he goes and searches for the one. And if the sheep in that famous parable may seem to be only a metaphor, then go on to the Gospel of Luke, where the principle is flatly set forth again, and where the sparrows stand, not for human beings, but for all creatures: "Are not five sparrows sold for two farthings, and not one of them is forgotten before God?" And John Donne had in mind a sort of equation and not a mere metaphor when he wrote, "If a clod be washed away by the sea, Europe is the less, as well as if a promontory were, as well as if a manor of thy friends or of thine own were; any man's death diminishes me . . ."

It is reassuring to see ecology moving toward a similar idea of the order of things. If an ecosystem loses one of its native species, we now know that we cannot speak of it as itself minus one species. An ecosystem minus one species is a different ecosystem. Just so, each of us is made by—or, one might better say, made as—a set of unique associations with unique persons, places, and things. The world of love does not admit the principle of the interchangeability of parts.

When John was in intensive care after his surgery, his wife, Carol, was standing by his bed, grieving and afraid. Wanting to reassure her, the nurse said, "Nothing is happening to him that doesn't happen to everybody."

And Carol replied, "I'm not everybody's wife."

In the world of love, things separated by efficiency and specialization strive to come back together. And yet love must confront death, and accept it, and learn from it. Only in confronting death can earthly love learn its true extent, its immortality. Any definition of health that is not silly must include death. The world of love includes death, suffers it, and triumphs over it. The world of efficiency is defeated by death; at death, all its instruments and procedures stop. The world of love continues, and of this, grief is the proof.

In the hospital, love cannot forget death. But, like love, death is in the hospital but not of it. Like love, fear and grief feel out of place in the hospital. How could they be included in its efficient procedures and mechanisms? Where a clear, small order is fervently maintained, fear and grief bring the threat of large disorder.

And so these two incompatible worlds might also be designated by the terms "amateur" and "professional"—amateur, in the literal sense of lover, one who participates for love; and professional, in the modern sense of one who performs highly specialized or technical procedures for pay. The amateur is excluded from the professional field.

For the amateur, in the hospital or in almost any other encounter with the medical industry, the overriding experience is that of being excluded from knowledge—of being unable, in other words, to make or participate in anything resembling an "informed decision." Of course, whether even doctors make informed decisions in the hospital is a matter of debate. For in the hospital even the professionals are involved in experience; experimentation has been left far behind. Experience, as all amateurs know, is not predictable, and in experience there are no replications or "controls;" there is nothing with which to compare the result. Once one decision has been made, we have destroyed the opportunity to know what would have happened if another decision had been made.

Still, in medicine, as in many modern disciplines, the amateur is divided from the professional by perhaps unbridgeable differences of knowledge and of language. An "informed decision" is really not even imaginable for most medical patients and their families, who have no competent understanding either of the patient's illness or the recommended medical or surgical procedure. Moreover, patients and their families are not likely to know the doctor, the surgeon, or any of the other people on whom the patient's life will depend. In the hospital, amateurs are more than likely to be proceeding entirely upon faith—and this is a peculiar and scary faith, for it must be placed, not in a god, but in mere people, mere procedures, mere chemicals, and mere machines.

It was only after my brother had been taken into surgery, I think, that the family understood the extremity of this deed of faith. We had decided—or John had decided and we had concurred—on the basis of the best advice available. But once he was separated from us, we felt the burden of our ignorance. We had not known what we were doing. One of our difficulties was the feeling that we had utterly given him up to what we did not know. And John spoke out of this sense of abandonment and helplessness in the intensive care unit after his surgery when he said, "I don't know what they're going to do to me or for me or with me."

As we waited and reports came at long intervals from the operating room, other realizations followed. We realized that, under the circumstances, we could not be told the truth. We would not know, ever, the worries and surprises that came to the surgeon during his work. We would not know the critical moments or the fears. If the surgeon did any part of his work ineptly or made a mistake, we would not know it. We realized, moreover that, if we were told the truth, we would have no way of knowing that the truth was what it was.

We realized that when the emissaries from the operating room assured us that everything was "normal" or "routine," they were referring to the procedure and not the patient. Even as amateurs—perhaps because we were amateurs—we knew that what was happening was not normal or routine for John or for us.

That these two worlds are as radically divided as they are does not mean that people cannot cross between them. I do not know how an amateur can cross over into the professional world; that does not seem very probable. But that professional people can cross back into the amateur world, I know from much evidence. During John's stay in the hospital there were many moments in which doctors and nurses—especially nurses!—allowed or caused the professional relationship to become a meeting between two human beings, and these moments were invariably moving.

The most moving, to me, happened in the waiting room during John's surgery. From time to time a nurse from the operating room would come to tell Carol what was happening. Carol, from politeness or bravery or both, always stood to receive the news, which, as I said, was always reassuring, and which always left us somewhat encouraged and somewhat doubtful. Carol's difficulty was that she had to suffer the ordeal not only as a wife but as one who had been a trained nurse. She knew, from her own education and experience, in how limited a sense open-heart surgery could be said to be normal or routine.

Finally, toward the end of our wait, two nurses came in. The operation, they said, had been a success. They explained again what had been done. And then they said that, after the completion of the bypasses, the surgeon had found it necessary to insert a "balloon pump" into the aorta to assist the heart. This possibility had never been mentioned, nobody was prepared for it, and Carol was sorely disappointed and upset. The two young women attempted to reassure her, mainly by repeating things they had already said. And then there was a long moment when they just looked at her. It was such a look as parents sometimes give to a sick or suffering child, when they themselves have begun to need the comfort they are trying to give.

And then one of the nurses said, "Do you need a hug?"

"Yes," Carol said.

And the nurse gave her a hug.

Which brings us to a starting place.

Birth Technology

MARY ANN LIESER

"I didn't get to ask my question," my friend said when I met her in the front row at the end of the question-and-answer period. "I wanted to ask them if they believe pregnancy and birth are normal and healthy."

It was a good question. Everything we had heard during the preceding two hours would lead a person to believe pregnancy is an illness and birth a perilous passage from which obstetricians must rescue both women and babies.

Curiosity had led me to attend that evening's program, an informational seminar sponsored by a local hospital and directed at women either pregnant now or planning to have a baby in the near future. Six doctors spoke in turn, each giving a short speech on his or her area of expertise, and afterward all six responded to questions from the audience. When it was all over, and people were beginning to leave the auditorium, I caught sight of some people I knew sitting in the front row.

My friend with the question that went unasked because time didn't allow her a turn during the question-and-answer period is a lay midwife. Her own five children were born at home. For the past half-dozen years she has helped several hundred other women birth their babies in the peace and dignity of their own homes. She was my midwife during my first pregnancy. Although she missed the birth itself (she was attending another birth and her assistant was with me), during the preceding nine months she helped me learn

68

that pregnancy and birth are indeed normal and healthy and can be accomplished with a minimum of technology.

This was not the message we heard from the doctors at that evening's program. What we did hear about over and over were all the things that we can find out about our unborn children, and all the ways we can control their passage into the world.

Amniocentesis is usually not performed until the sixteenth week of pregnancy, so doctors have long been working on the development of diagnostic tests that can be performed earlier. Chorionic villi sampling (CVS), which involves the removal of one of the microscopic fingerlike vessels that reach into the umbilical wall and eventually form the placenta, can now be done at eight weeks. Another new procedure is percutaneous umbilical blood sampling (PUBS), in which an instrument penetrates the uterine wall to draw blood at the site where the umbilical cord joins the placenta. All these procedures carry some risk of infection, hemorrhage, and miscarriage. The latter two procedures are also suspected to increase the risk of certain birth defects. Often, women are convinced to submit to such testing in order to be reassured that their babies are normal and healthy. Sadly, every year some women miscarry healthy fetuses or give birth to babies with birth defects as a result of the tests they underwent to determine the health of the unborn child.

In fact, one of the questions that did get asked at that evening's program concerned the wisdom of performing such tests. "Why add even a small risk?" one man inquired. The doctor's answer was that the problems for which they screen are of higher risk than are the tests themselves. He meant that, for example, a woman over the age of thirty-five is more likely to be carrying a child with Down's syndrome than she is likely to miscarry a normal baby as a result of having amniocentesis. This comparison, of Down's syndrome versus death, is statistically true. But I don't believe I would look at it in such a way if I were that over-thirty-five woman.

I believe one reason doctors encourage prenatal diagnostic testing is their fear of birth and of death. This fearfulness is indeed part of the very fabric of our contemporary culture, and it drives us to do more tests, to gather more information. The more we know, the more we can control; the more we are in control, the more we can avoid that which we fear. But it doesn't always work out so neatly. Our attempts to control what we were never meant to control have steered us to scenarios that are much more frightening.

The majority of pregnant women in this country now undergo at least one ultrasound scan. In many obstetric practices this procedure is a routine screening performed on every woman. Some women even ask for an ultrasound so they can keep as a souvenir a picture of the unborn child inside their womb. This happens despite the fact that ultrasound has never been demonstrated to be absolutely safe. Even the American College of Obstetricians and Gynecologists recommends ultrasound be used only when medically indicated, but many obstetric practices ignore that guideline when setting up their own protocol. How long will it be—how many babies will be exposed in utero to ultrasound—before the risk or benignity of the procedure is finally determined? It took decades for researchers to learn that diethylstilbestrol (DES) caused genetic defects in the reproductive systems of women whose mothers were exposed to this drug during pregnancy. It took decades because those defects didn't show up until the daughters of DES-exposed women were adults themselves.

All of the women who took DES during the decades it was prescribed were assured by their physicians and the FDA that it was perfectly safe. But it was not.

Is ultrasound the DES of the future? I don't know. It may well be a harmless procedure in the long run, but why take the risk that it's not? Why expose virtually every pregnant woman and unborn baby? Such a level of medical testing makes sense only in a culture that is more afraid of death, and thus of life, than of anything else.

At that evening's program it was clear to me that the doctors who spoke carry with them a great deal of fear, which colors their view of everything surrounding birth. They endlessly seek more knowledge so they can control what they fear. Over and over I heard phrases such as "exciting new test," "exciting advances," "we've gotten a lot smarter," and "we want to find out all we can." One doctor went so far as to say that her goal is to be able to guarantee a healthy baby to every mother. Another spoke of "scripting" the baby's birth to "create just what you want."

While birthing women should be making choices about what they want, no one mentioned that of course we can't create "just what we want," because we aren't the creators at birth. No one mentioned that the reason doctors cannot guarantee a healthy baby to every mother is that ultimately it is not in our control to do so, and was never meant to be. We are not gods.

In *Open Season*, Nancy Wainer Cohen writes:

> "Birth, like death, is not fully controllable. We weren't meant to understand birth or to control it. We are meant to take responsibility for the parts of it that we can, and then just experience it. . . . At some point, we must let go and allow the process to be. Faith is not belief without proof but trust without reservation."

I believe another reason many doctors encourage women to undergo all the diagnostic testing available is because they themselves are convinced that pregnancy is not normal and healthy. Unfortunately, they also convince the women in their care of this idea, and thus undermine the women's confidence in their own ability to give birth.

Despite all the supposed relaxation of hospital delivery practices—the birthing suites, nurse-midwifery programs, and hospital-sponsored childbirth classes—*more* women giving birth in hospitals are receiving pain medication now than twenty years ago. Many labor and give birth with IV tubes inserted in a vein on their forearm so they'll be ready, just in case they have to go to surgery. Lamentably, at least one in five do end up undergoing a cesarean section. Most of these cesareans are unnecessary; all involve increased risk to both mother and baby. The majority of birthing women are hooked up at some point to an electronic fetal monitor (EFM), an ultrasound device that is strapped over a woman's abdomen and gives a printout of the mother's contractions and the baby's heartbeat. Originally developed soley for high-risk births, fetal monitoring has rapidly become routine for all women in many hospitals, although many times the monitor readings are difficult to interpret. The number of cesarean sections rises as birth attendants panic over readings they don't understand.

Birth becomes more impersonal, as well. Many women have complained that once they were hooked up to a fetal monitor, the nurses never looked them in the eye again, but just came in the room to look at the monitor printout. Even the American College of Obstetricians and Gynecologists admits that periodically listening to the baby's heartbeat with a fetoscope (a stethoscope-like instrument that rests on a pregnant woman's belly and has earpieces for listening to the baby's heartbeat) is as effective as electronic fetal monitoring. But after twenty years of monitoring, many nurses and doctors have forgotten how to use a fetoscope. Some never learned.

As we increasingly rely on technology, we ourselves become

more and more helpless. Who will remember how to use a feto-scope? Who will remember how to gently guide a baby into our world without sophisticated equipment? Chances are, most of those who will remember will be midwives. Their hearts and their hands are their most important tools. Midwives, particularly those who attend home births, carry and practice the memory of what birth can be like without unnecessary technology. After all, women's bodies are uniquely designed and adapted to birth their own babies. Babies, too, are designed and adapted to be born the way nature intended.

The most ironic consequence of all our efforts to make birth safe is that we've made it more dangerous. Studies show that for a healthy pregnant woman the safest place to have a baby is at home with a midwife in attendance.* Among groups of women matched for age, income level, and risk factors, those who choose a home birth experience significantly fewer deaths, infections, and complications, and their babies have lower mortality rates and a lower incidence of birth defects, as well. The effort to control what we fear has backfired.

Every form of technology brings a load of baggage with it. Some of the baggage may be long-term risks or harmful consequences that no one knows about or bothers to notice in the first giddy rush to embrace something new. Much of the baggage consists of social consequences. People are intimately affected by the introduction into their lives of a new technology. The whole complex web of how people relate to each other is also affected. Seldom are any of these factors discussed before the technology is adopted.

---

*Many studies comparing hospital and home birth outcomes are collected in Henci Goer, *Obstetric Myths Versus Research Realities: A Guide to Medical Literature* (Westport, Conn.: Bergin & Garvey, 1995) and in the writings of former World Health Organization official Marsden Wagner, M.D., *Pursuing the Birth Machine: The Search for Appropriate Birth Technology* (Campersdown, NSW, Australia: ACE Graphics, 1994).

What, then, are some of the consequences for our society of our overreliance on birth technology? By making technology and tools central to birth for even the most healthy and low-risk mothers, we have left little or no room for the human touch. In many cases, those who attend births in hospitals have forgotten how to use their hearts and their hands. What could be an empowering experience for women often leaves them feeling victimized. What should be a deeply moving spiritual experience, we are numb to. The technological environment results in babies born in distress, who are then "saved" from the results of all the interventions their mothers suffered during labor. The doctors take credit for "saving" the baby, but not for causing the problems in the first place. Babies end up separated from their mothers during their first hours and days of life, when they most need to be gently welcomed to this world by those who love them.

Saying "no" to birth technology, stepping outside the medical model, and reclaiming our own power to birth our babies in our own way can be radical and healing to the soul. My own two births were very different from each other. One was long; one was over quickly. One involved hours of patient pushing; the other found us praying the midwife would arrive before the baby. One took place in the early night after an all-day labor; the other just before dawn, after we'd spent most of the night sleeping as usual. One was a week before my due date; the other was—by the medical calendar anyway— late. At both births, however, I felt the presence of God as I have at no other time. And I did not feel fear. I knew that, ultimately, I was not in control.

The most tragic consequence of our overreliance on birth technology is that it often leaves no room for God. I am convinced that birth is one of the times God intends to enter our lives most directly. Our drive to control what we fear leaves no opening for our Creator.

The Giver and Taker of Lives

DAVID AND ELIZABETH VENDLEY

An oil lamp quietly burns, giving a soft light to the corner room of a small house. An extraordinary event is about to take place: a baby will soon be born. The scene is calm. Mom, midwife, and helper are waiting for Dad to come in from chores. He comes, and quickly leaves his bucket of milk on the counter, washes up, and changes clothes in a hurry. He is not in the room long before his seventh child is born, a girl. Many prayers rise up from the room, as they have throughout the night. Soon the other children are awake and happily surprised to be greeted with the sight of Mom in bed holding their new baby sister.

This is not a scene from the early part of the century; it happened last fall. Not in some remote and isolated cabin, but in a densely populated community. The people were at home by choice, not because they couldn't get to the hospital. They were at home because, by the grace of God, they did not need a hospital. Had something gone amiss, they would not have hesitated to go to the hospital.

We are grateful for that choice. Yes, this story is about our family. We have been blessed to be able to have our last three babies at home.

We would be deceptive, however, to leave the scene at this peaceful point. The fact is that soon after the birth, our sixteen-month-old

son was the focus of attention. The previous evening he had taken a nasty fall and was in obvious need of medical evaluation. The timing was awful, to say the least. A paramedic friend monitored him through the night, and this allowed us to feel sure he was fairly stable until we were in a better position to get him to a doctor. The remainder of the day for Dad was quite a contrast from the start; no quiet barn, no softly lit corners of the house. He found himself in the stainless-steel ordered routine of modern medical technology. And as he watched his little son move through the massive CT scanner, he could only shake his head at the contrast between the two situations. The fall his child had taken could have—logically should have—caused death. But God had other plans. He gave our family two lives in one day.

Along with striving to live a plain life, free of the world and its trappings, we face a question: Where do we draw the line? One of the toughest places to discern this, in our opinion, is concerning medical treatment. We will freely admit that we ourselves have yet to develop a mature, consistent medical philosophy for our family. At the same time, we do feel in control of this area of our lives rather than being controlled by the medical establishment.

Our personal way of thinking as Christians differs greatly from the attitudes and assumptions of medical orthodoxy. One of the main underlying themes of the medical establishment would be a good example. To the medical profession, physical death is an enemy to be avoided and expunged at all costs. It is such a frightening prospect that some doctors are willing to go to ridiculous lengths to avoid it. As Christians, we are not so very attached to our earthly lives. Our heavenly hope is the next stop after our heart and lungs cease to function. What sweeter comfort can we have than the thought of resting forever in our Savior's arms, beholding His face—joy unspeakable!

We see God as the giver and taker of lives. He has willed us here, and we feel we are to keep our bodies as a gift would be cared for. Scripture admonishes us to keep ourselves holy and pure, free of corruption. To one Christian, corruption in bodily terms may mean eating a fast-food hamburger, where another draws the line at cigarettes, alcohol, and drugs. For our family it is a process of careful monitoring of the things on, in, and with regard to our bodies. It is our goal to treat these earthly vessels with respect for the awesome Power in whose image they were created. And when the end of our earthly lives does come, we hope to be found undefiled in both body and spirit.

Another modern idea is that life here ought to be perfect or at least very, very close to perfect. Our courts are jam-packed with civil suits because a product was not labeled with enough cautions or a surgery did not end up effective. So we as a society have moved our standards higher and higher and now expect to be free of all inconveniences including physical discomfort. A limp that was barely noticed twenty years ago is now grounds for a full-blown joint replacement. Our mechanized mind-set tells us to go in and fix the broken part, troubleshoot, understand it all.

Realistically, though, we can't understand it all, for we are fearfully and wonderfully made. Made by a Creator so far superior to us that our best medical breakthroughs are a speck of dust compared to the awesome truth of how He created our bodies to work. From that fateful day in the Garden forward, innocence, physical perfection, and freedom from discomfort have all been beyond our grasp. Just as we accept work as part of our existence, so must we accept illness and, by the grace of God, death.

It seems the main premises of the medical profession are contrary to our fundamental beliefs. They would say death is an awful thing; perfection is the goal; we can (and will) eventually understand it all. Our truth is that physical death is our entrance to eternal life in Christ Jesus; life until then will involve pain and suffering; and we can never wholly comprehend the wondrous way in which we are made.

So there we are at the start—at total odds with the medical community. But unlike many aspects of modern life, we do need to interact with the medical establishment to some degree. Just like cash in the money economy, some medical care must be used for expediency and practicality's sake. But to what degree? Where do we draw the line?

A situation we find ourselves in often is that of facing decisions concerning pharmaceuticals. We are more than a little cautious about dipping our toes in this often consuming whirlpool. More than once we have seen an earache go from one medication to two additional medications due to the side effects of the first, only to have all three conditions reappear once the chemical bombardment is stopped. Surely there must be a gentler way to handle a condition that has only a 15 percent chance of not resolving itself on its own. The hard part comes in knowing on which side of the percentile you are going to land.

This is where we feel the better-safe-than-sorry blanket gets thrown over all earaches by the medical profession. To us it sort of seems like scrubbing the entire floor to remove one glob of spilled jelly; shouldn't we first try a dab of soap on a dishrag before risking a bleach burn over the whole floor? For us, even after seven children, it is hard to decide which episodes call for a doctor and which do not. But it is getting better, and we are surprised at how often the situation needs greater patience rather than medical intervention. We do not feel confident enough to advise someone not to see a doctor. But we can say there is a choosing point of how much the doctor has to be a part of your life.

As for earaches, our methods involve treatment with herbs that stimulate *natural* body functions, along with time-tested grandma-style remedies. This seems like a calmer route to us and has proven effective in most cases. When it isn't enough we are willing to go to the doctor and follow his plan, if that is what we asked him for.

While we are asking for the services of a doctor, we owe his or her treatment respectful consideration. However, there are also immense consequences for all involved when we give total mindless obedience to what the doctor says. Most doctors desire plenty of input from us and feel best about their course of treatment when they have engaged in a thorough dialogue with us about the options. If you doubt your doctors feel this way, ask them. Their answers may very well help you see whether or not you have the right doctors for your family's needs.

The points we have made here regarding the medical establishment versus our own views are not comprehensive or exhaustive. Neither is it our intention to be a forum for our point of view, but rather to illustrate a few factors we have taken into consideration over the years in our ongoing process of establishing our own family medical philosophy. The issues are mostly of control, but also of safety and cost (we could write another essay on cost alone). Searching for that spot to draw the line seems to be an ongoing process. Each situation calls for a balancing act and prayerful consideration.

For example, we are all for home birth, but that is an easy thing to be when you are only twelve miles from a hospital and fifty yards from a phone. Another consideration we are now heeding is the level of prayer we are using. We are so accustomed to simply reaching for that bottle of acetaminophen or cough syrup that we now have to stop ourselves and ask, Have I made this a matter of prayer? Am I guilty of trusting this medicine before God? Once we are sure we have considered the Lord's point of view, it is easier and less stressful to choose from the options. As you can see, we are still growing and searching in this area ourselves.

When we look back on that roller coaster of a day last fall we wonder, Should we have just not taken our son to the doctor? After all, our little boy turned out to be all right with just simple tender loving care at home and a couple weeks of recuperation. In hindsight perhaps all would have been fine, but from a safety standpoint the risk was too high. Yes, he received better care because of the CT scan, because the quick results meant we were then able to bring him home rather than endure a hospital stay for observation. And as for his baby sister, well, she has a whole story of her own on this topic, and will most probably provide us with many more ups and downs on the issue before we are finished. So it is our intention to move soberly and watchfully forward, learning and leaning as we go.

Food We Can Live With

Art Gish

Food and Community

I live and work as a member of a small Christian intentional community where we daily share our lives together, including working together growing organic vegetables as our main source of income. Producing food is a community activity. Growing food is one way we share our lives together.

Yesterday we planted the sweet potatoes and eggplants. The children and adults worked together in the rain, trying to get all those tender plants in the ground before it became too wet. We all got soaked and muddy, but that was fun. A week ago we all planted lots of peppers, and this week we have loads of asparagus, peas, and rhubarb to harvest. Yum, yum! And besides sustaining us with food and income, taking these vegetables to market brings us together with the people around us.

Raising food for people is a holy and sacred calling. To provide food that is healthy and nutritious is a sign of our stewardship of the gift of life. Instead of using more technology and fossil fuels, we have chosen ways of growing food that are labor intensive. Instead of decreasing human labor and increasing fossil energy input, we seek to decrease the use of that energy and increase the ways we can work together. We still feel the need to use a small tractor for some garden work, but we certainly know that the tractor doesn't help bring us together.

What we are striving for is an intimate relationship with the soil, the plants, and with each other. There is a strong connection between how we relate to the soil and how we relate to one another. It follows that the ideology of control and domination so integral to the conduct of agribusiness is something we want to put behind us.

So we turn to planting, hoeing, harvesting, selling, preserving—all communal activities, ways we share our lives with each other. Soon we will be harvesting the garlic. Cleaning all that garlic is a lot of work, but sitting in a circle in the shade of a July afternoon makes the whole activity a lot of fun.

Getting ready for market is a big deal with us. Picking, washing, packing, loading onto the truck—it all takes a good deal of effort. Doing it together makes it seem much easier. I would not want to farm if I had to do it alone.

In contrast to our community's methods, it must be said that much of the food available today has been grown in horribly oppressive conditions. Think of the farmworkers (slaves?) in Central America who work for pennies a day so we can have cheap bananas. Or factory farms where animals endure a miserable existence, such as chickens whose feet grow fast to the small cages in which they are imprisoned so we can have cheap eggs. Or the enormous use of chemicals to mass-produce low-quality food with all its destructive effects on soil and water.

Can we begin to think about the ethical issues involved in eating those bananas, eggs, and meat? Is buying these products in effect voting for the continuation of these practices? Do our buying patterns support big agribusiness and the destruction of small farms? Is the cheapest price the best choice in the long run?

Food can be produced in a healthy, sustainable way. Distribution of that food can also be a healthy process, helping to bring people together. Distribution in this sense means sharing our food with others. It would be nice not to have to charge money for our vegetables. On the other hand, by paying us, our customers are sharing with us and supporting us. And we can give much more than food in return for money.

What a gift it is, after all, to have a personal relationship with the people who grow your food, to know where it comes from, how it was raised, and who raised it! This may include visiting the farm where your food comes from. Our customers are welcome to visit our farm and make an even stronger connection with both us and the methods by which their food is grown.

At the farmer's market, every day brings new opportunities for sharing, for catching up with friends, for strengthening ties of friendship, for supporting each other. We value and treasure these relationships. Our market does more than distribute fresh, locally grown, wholesome food. It is a social, cultural event that brings many of the people of our area together.

I watch with joy as I see so many relationships renewed, strengthened, and even being formed right in front of our stand. Those relationships are incredibly important to building a cohesive culture that can sustain people with more than food.

Conversely, there isn't much community inside a big supermarket. There, we shop as isolated individuals, each in our own private world. Gone are the relationships with the soil, the grower, and, for the most part, even the distributor. Do you know the name of the produce manager in your supermarket? Or anything about his or her family?

Efficiency? Yes. Community? No. Even the supposed efficiency of the supermarket is largely an illusion. The average bite of food eaten in the United States is transported somewhere around two thousand miles. That is hardly sustainable, either in terms of the energy needed for that transportation, or in the severing of the bonds between consumers, producers, and the soil.

Food in the modern system also doesn't get distributed very evenly. While many people starve or go to bed hungry, others bask in opulence. We waste incredible amounts of food. Check the

Dumpster behind any supermarket or restaurant and you will be amazed at all the waste. Then add to that all the food we leave on our plates at home.

There is no shortage of food in the world. The only reason most people are hungry is that they do not have the resources to produce or buy food. If this is the case, then it should be obvious that concentrating resources of land and wealth into the hands of fewer and fewer people will lead to increasing hunger. The current system of industrialized farming and mass distribution furthers this process.

The Meaning of Food

Eating three meals a day with each other in our intentional community is an important part of our life together. Each meal includes singing, praying, sharing, laughing, and serving each other. The visits of our guests seem incomplete if we don't eat at least one meal with them. I even joke that we can't worship together unless we first eat together.

The best part about food, of course, is eating it. That is, if we eat it with others. Eating alone isn't very much fun.

The consumption of food implies celebration, neighborliness, generosity, thanksgiving, community. Think about feasts, festivals, potlucks, communal meals; the best thing about eating is not the food, but the fellowship around the table.

How different this is than eating at McDonald's! Gone are any relationships with even those who serve us. Our eating there may involve gluttony, but it is hardly a feast, and goes to prove that eating is not always a good thing. One of the reasons one-third of North Americans are severely overweight is that we eat too much! Gluttony is a problem for many of us.

We also eat lots of food that is unhealthy. Should we be eating so much fat, meat, sugar, white flour, and salt? To what extent are increasing rates of cancer, heart disease, and immune deficiencies the result of eating so much unhealthy food?

Plain living involves good eating. We can have the best of locally grown food, prepare it simply, and eat it joyously and gratefully. It is hardly a sacrifice to eat more fruits and vegetables, more whole grains. We need only compare whole-grain breads with the white fluffy stuff they sell at the convenience store to know this.

Today, an often neglected aspect of eating is its opposite—fasting. Fasting can also be a treat. It can be a time of cleansing and rest for our bodies. But more importantly, fasting can be a form of discipline and prayer. If undertaken in the right spirit, we can find in fasting a new freedom from a life of addiction.

Before you take another bite of food, ask where it came from, and whether it was raised and delivered to you in accordance with God's intentions for the earth.

Food is important. Sometimes too important—some people live to eat instead of eating to live. But food is important. Let's ask questions about food: How many thousand miles has our food been moved? What chemicals were used to produce it? What does the food do to our bodies? How does it taste? Were people oppressed in the process of producing it? Was the land degraded? What impact did the methods of production and distribution have on relationships? Did it foster or destroy community?

And what, exactly, is the center of our community? What sustains it? Is it a big supermarket chain, the petrochemical industry, the shopping malls? Or is our community to be found in the network of relationships in which we know and support one another? What place does food have in that community?

If, in community, we find respect, nurturance, relationships, integrity, wisdom, and reverence, while the opposite of community is abuse, control, domination, and desecration, then where does our food fit into this scheme? How does our eating contribute to community or support the destruction of community?

———

A first-century radical named Jesus put it well: He said not to worry about what we will eat or drink. He then compared us to birds. They are fed and taken care of. Aren't we as valuable as they are? he asked.

Instead of worrying about what we will eat, Jesus suggested that we first seek God's community. Then everything else will find its proper perspective.

Working

When we married, Mary Ann and I had a combined income of about $65,000 (in 1998 money) plus health benefits. That amount seems like a small fortune to us now. Eight years and four children later, our family of six now achieves the basics of life with a salary of about one-third of what we started with. But I was about $16,000 in debt back then, all since repaid. Today we have nicer, handmade clothes. We eat better food. All of these things feel to us like upward mobility, where the upward has some true meaning.

It has all come about because our family is beginning to learn the art of sharing with our neighbors and friends. With the help of community, we are slowly leaving more and more of the global economy out of our private accounting. By letting go of all that we once thought we could not live without, Mary Ann and I have discovered there is an unexpected gift waiting. We haven't just left the global economy; we aren't heroic individualists going it alone. We have, instead, come into the economy of loving and mutual obligation. We may not be able to explain what is so pleasing about this new relationship, but as David Kline puts it in his essay "The Value of Love" dealing in this economy "just seems right."

Leaving Money Behind

BILL DUESING

My relationship with money has certainly been checkered. It is variable and slippery stuff and exerts a powerful and often destructive force. Diminishing the importance of money in our lives is a worthwhile goal.

Our family has not yet been able to leave the money economy, and we aren't likely to do so anytime soon. However, by bartering, doing with less for ourselves, spending money more carefully and locally (whenever possible), as well as by learning to pay less attention to price, we have reduced the role of money. These strategies have enriched our lives.

One day in the middle of last winter, our friend Gary called and asked if we needed any firewood. I thought that this offer was a part of our ongoing barter arrangement, which I didn't really feel I was owed. Because the winter had been so mild and we still had some wood left (although most of it wasn't quite dry or needed further processing), I was tempted to tell him not to bother. Gary had to travel at least twenty miles to deliver this wood to us, but he was determined, so I said, "Great."

A day or two later, the weather changed and we had an extended stretch of very cold, wintry weather. That half cord of split, dry hardwood Gary delivered (and insisted we stack right by the back door) turned out to be very necessary to get us through a particularly cold time when we were also quite busy with our off-farm educational work.

The timely firewood delivery was in return for half a pig we'd given his family. But he'd helped us cut up and wrap two pigs and brought in a cash customer, so I figured we were even. In years past, Gary has raised chickens and turkeys. We helped with their slaughter and, in return, got birds for our freezer.

Gary and I have been bartering, without calling it that, since the early 1970s when he taught me how to roof condominiums so I could earn the money I needed to pay for land I'd just bought, and so that he could take a vacation. Gary was a country boy, connected to farming by birth, and a recent graduate of the University of Connecticut's agriculture program. I'd been raised in the city and was new to the country. I brought lots of ideas about organic agriculture and planting trees with me.

Gary and I have been sharing knowledge and enthusiasm—and helping each other—ever since. Even though we see each other only two or three times a year now, we still have an active relationship based on sharing. While I was writing this essay, he called to arrange a trade of our garlic for his blueberries.

We have also evolved a complex barter arrangement with some closer neighbors. Robert provides computer advice and repairs, and Cynthia removes poison ivy from places around our house. In return we trade pork, eggs, potatoes, and a garden plot on our farm.

In both these arrangements, the exchanges are based more on friendship and mutual sharing of resources than on any particular accounting of value. They are ongoing and open-ended; they provide the mortar that cements our community together.

There are added values when we produce goods and services for barter or for ourselves. The fruits of our labor are, in effect, tax-free income. Our gardens, kitchens, woodlots, south-facing windows, and shade trees provide not only valuable goods and service, they also add texture and depth to our lives. They allow a small amount of money spent for seeds, tools, or glass, for example, and some of our labor, to produce food and comfort.

The vegetables we grow and eat, the solar energy flowing through our south windows in the winter, the cooling shade of large trees, dry clothes from the line, as well as the pleasure we take in talking with family and friends around the dinner table, are all forms of tax-free income. To buy the goods we are replacing—vegetables from California, oil from Kuwait, electricity from the nuclear power plant, propane from a New Jersey refinery, and electronic entertainment from Hollywood—we have to earn enough to pay income, sales, and other taxes and still have enough left to purchase the product or service. At average rates, we have to earn one dollar in order to purchase about sixty cents' worth of vegetables or energy. To earn that amount of money often requires more money to be spent to commute or to buy special clothes, for example. When we think in this way, the monetary value of homegrown lettuce, home-made entertainment, and sun-warmed rooms increases dramatically. There is an appropriate justice in this reckoning. Food, entertainment, and energy from distant sources have already consumed enormous amounts of tax dollars as subsidies that enable them to seem so cheap in the marketplace. If you want to put a monetary value on the root-cellared produce from your garden, look at the store price of organic onions and potatoes in the winter, and add the cost of getting to the store.

The pleasures of the garden or living in a sun-filled house in January, the improved freshness, flavor, and nutrition of homegrown food, the wonderful aroma of sun-dried clothes, and the benefits of family talk add priceless value to the work we do at home.

Producing our own also gives us a good sense of the true cost of things. When we grow our own vegetables, we know there must have been some corners cut, costs hidden, and subsidies provided in order to sell us ten-cents-per-pound potatoes and cheap California lettuce.

Once we understand this, prices will become less important. One of the primary articles of faith in our society is that a lower price is better. But the low price is often artificial and designed to put a store or farmer with more realistic prices out of business. If we drive past our local store to get a "better deal" at the giant discount chain, we condemn ourselves to fewer choices once the local store is out of business, and to spending more time in our cars. Ultimately, we diminish the integrity of our community.

Price is often a lie that comes with enormous hidden costs. Cigarettes, pesticides, land mines, gasoline, and junk food epitomize this phenomenon with their low purchase prices and very high, long-term costs to society.

The way we spend or invest our money does make a difference. The dominant culture says, "It doesn't matter. Just spend money and look for the lowest price. Just invest your money and look for the highest yield." When we give our money to people who do good work and provide a worthwhile product, we sustain them. When we spend money in our communities, we support our communities. We encourage businesses that are important to us. They are usually the ones whose owners actually work in the business themselves and live right in town.

We also benefit by not buying products from, or investing in, large corporations, especially those that destroy forests or push cigarettes, cars, junk food, infant formula, weapons, pesticides, or nuclear power. With the incredible range of products pouring out from many of these large corporations, this informal boycott compels us to change our habits and to make do with less. As we discover that there are fewer places to spend our money, our need for bartering and doing for ourselves increases. We find that there are fewer places to invest our money and feel good about it. We realize that having more money is actually a burden. Our need for money diminishes.

There is another reason for spending money in our local communities. In spite of what global money traders would like us to believe, money's value is really local in time and space. For example, one dollar had vastly different values in 1890 and in 1990, as it has vastly different values now in New York City and in a rural village in India. Just the last few years have provided numerous examples of drastic changes in the dollar value of real estate and foreign currencies. Our son Dan was in India last winter studying sustainable communities as part of his college education. He brought back some beautiful cloth, handwoven of hand-spun cotton, for which he paid about $1.25 per yard. In sharp contrast, helping a neighbor build his house this summer, Dan makes enough every ten minutes to buy another yard of that labor- and skill-intensive cloth!

The exploitation of these and other less dramatic differences by global traders is a cause of much hardship in the world. It wreaks havoc with aspects of human lives that have unchanging values—a loved and loving mate, a productive garden, a viable community, or a nourishing family meal. Money can, however, have a fairly consistent value within a community. This is why local currencies such as "Hours" in Ithaca, New York, and "Berkshares" in western Massachusetts (with a value based on a cord of dry hardwood) hold so much promise. In the Berkshires resort area, hordes of vacationing New Yorkers (with their big-city dollars) interact with a much less affluent local population. "Berkshares," which can only be spent locally, are one way of mediating this difference.

During my life, the times I have had little money taught me very valuable lessons about how to do without it and what's important about it. The (very) few periods when I had a relatively large amount of money were disastrous. Having a number of regular sources of small amounts of money, for doing work I believe in, seems a good balance.

Find sources of happiness that don't depend on money. Family, gardens, worship, community, nature, pleasant and relevant work, and health can help us detach from and lessen our reliance on money for the truly important things.

To diminish the importance of money in our lives (to somehow seek a balance) is a real challenge. By appreciating the value of those things that can't be bought with money and understanding the connections and effects of the money we do spend, we'll be on the way to putting money in its place: a useful medium of exchange in our local community with a powerfully destructive role on a larger scale.

The Value of Love

DAVID KLINE

Farming has fallen on tough times, especially the small-scale, diversified, noncontract livestock farms the Amish in this part of the country (Holmes County, Ohio) prefer. Hog prices recently hit a thirty-year low point; cull cow prices are scraping bottom, and milk prices, the mainstay of the community, are down. Our neighbor told me that for his July milk he received the lowest prices in thirteen years. (This low milk price is surely due in large part to the FDA approval of bovine growth hormone, a synthetic hormone invented by Monsanto that, when injected into cows, stimulates them to produce more milk—milk we do not need. So we farmers are paying for Monsanto's sins.)

One benefit, however, of these depressed farm prices is that I have become even more keenly aware of how important is the help of my neighbors in making farming profitable. I am referring to that exchange of labor where no money is involved; I never carry my wallet or checkbook when working on neighboring farms because I'm always paying back with my labor what they have already done, or will do, for me.

This moneyless exchange often involves more than labor. It can be a sharing of machinery and knowledge or even an exchange of fertility. One year we had more third-cutting hay than we needed and the field was almost too far away to graze, so we made a deal with our neighbor who was in need of more hay. He got the six acres of hay, probably around two hundred bales, and in turn he spread six loads of manure on that field and we got a free service to his draft-horse stud.

In our neighborhood exchange of labor we never keep close account of the hours we trade. It usually goes by a half or a full day's work. Last fall, for instance, I helped one neighbor run his shocks of corn through the mechanical corn husker and shredder. So he still owes me a day of labor, which will be used helping me put up a new line fence. We both know that good fences make good neighbors. Besides, he has a power posthole digger that we will use to bore the holes for the new posts. So, when the cost of his equipment is figured in, he will be doing more for me than I did for him with my manual labor. But I know when we are finished with the fence, and we both look at it with satisfaction, he will insist that we are now fair and square.

A lot of this exchange is tied to the biblical references of "love thy neighbor as thyself," and "do unto others as ye would have them do unto thee." And the belief that your neighbor is your neighbor whether he attends your church or is an unbeliever. So I help him and he helps me. We need each other.

This love for your neighbor was clearly pointed out to me a few years ago when an elderly farmer from our community died. His family lived at the far end of our school district, and his wish was to be buried in the neighborhood cemetery instead of the cemetery of their church district. He said he wants to be with the people he spent most of his time with: his neighbors who made it possible for him to farm in a low-cost way with their labor, the people who were always there when he needed them, and with whom he laughed and hunted and shared wonderful meals. Of course, he was a generous man and helped his neighbors much in return.

How much does this free labor mean to us farmers economically? Probably much more than we realize, because we are so used to it. For one, I know it enables us to harvest our crops with a minimal amount of machinery and fossil-fuel use.

This summer we found out, in a small way. In our real horse-powered agriculture, oats are still an important crop. Important first as horse feed, the oats are also used in hog and chicken feed and for the dairy cows. And in the winter we eat rolled oats for breakfast.

In any case, when a severe summer storm threatens, especially around mid-June when the oats are "heading out" and at their most vulnerable for lodging, our first thoughts are "Oh no, the oats!" This past summer was angst-ridden oatswise. Our field endured four major thunderstorms. From the four directions. The first, from the east, also had hail. By the time the fourth one, from the west, was finished, our oats—and our hopes—were flattened.

The crop was beyond cutting with a binder, so we hired a custom operator with his combine to harvest the oats. For ten acres it cost $225. Plus the grain was too wet to store so we hired someone to dry it. Another $180. In a storm-free year the crop could have been harvested with the free labor of my neighbors and ten dollars' worth of fuel. As the saying goes, What we don't spend is profit.

There is also a savings of money beyond the direct exchange of labor, and that is in multiuse equipment. This week the last silo in our silo-filling ring was filled. The Weavers had planted some corn late, and it wasn't ready to be ensiled here until late in September. Seven wagons and men worked together picking up bundles of corn. The wagons and teams are the same ones we use for hay making, threshing, wood and apple hauling, taking the schoolchildren from one school to another for a game of softball on pleasant fall afternoons, and dozens of other jobs around the farm. No special or expensive equipment is needed to fill our silos.

Most of us do possess our own silo filler, an archaic machine that is fairly inexpensive and not cumbersome to store. Plus most have a corn binder, a 1940s machine that cuts the corn and ties it (most of the time) into bundles. The binder is also used to cut dried-down corn when its fodder is needed for the livestock's winter bedding. So it, too, is not a single-purpose machine.

Seven wagons and teamsters, each picking up bundles of corn and loading them on the wagons in this perfect weather of September when the crispness of the night kept our coats on for the first load—this was labor exchange at its finest. Conditions were so ideal that not to feel good about it would have been impossible, at least in my opinion.

As the sun warmed the morning air, coats were thrown aside, and migrating turkey vultures and red-tailed hawks began leaning into nothingness, searching for the rising updrafts, to ride the invisible towers of heated air into the cobalt autumn sky. Monarch butterflies drifted southwest on their long journey to the Sierra Madre mountains in Mexico. Blue jays scolded. Crows called.

For a month, since filling the first silo in late August, we had been working together. Not every day, of course, but about two days each week. This last day the Percheron teams outnumbered the Belgians, for the farm was along the township road that the draft-horse people affectionately call Percheron Alley. The mood of the crew was lively; talk flowed freely in the field and even more so around the dinner table as the farm economy was discussed, the low milk prices, how hog prices are slowly rebounding. Best of all were the stories—stories, some tragic, some humorous, that are retold annually.

But this exchange of labor is also more than monetary; I detected it around that dinner table. It is the good feeling of helping your neighbor. It just seems right. Words tend to fail me when attempting to describe the sensation.

It reminds me of a river—serene and beautiful—yet within its gentle flow is great strength. But that power is not a controlling force; it is peaceful and satisfying. There is a security in working beyond the grips of the money economy. As I unloaded the last load and looked out across the fertile valley, over the crowns of the cottonwoods and willows along the creek, at the farms we worked on this past month, and at our farm in the distance, I sighed with gratitude for the blessing of living in a neighborhood where sharing labor is a work of love.

Building a Faithful Home

MARK KORBAN

The summer of 1995 was a string of hot, dry days in the northeast U.S. They say it was one of the driest on record. Not good for the dairy farms in Vermont near the Canadian border, but well suited to our task: building a house of straw bales and covering it with cement stucco. We needed to have the house complete enough to move into by the time the cold weather hit in October, so each day counted. We missed only one day due to rain, and the straw bales stayed dry until they were permanently protected under two layers of cement.

Two Orthodox monks and a deacon, his wife, and family of five children made the daily trek from the Holy Transfiguration Skete in nearby Quebec. The monks had graciously offered to house us in some spare rooms of the monastery while building, and to help us do the building for the entire summer. Since we were operating on a shoestring budget of $12,000, their help largely made the task possible.

The plan for the house was the result of more than architectural considerations. It was also the fruit of many years of thought and trial in an attempt to apply the gospel of Christ to all aspects of our daily lives. We approached the design of the house as we try to approach all of life, by asking, How does one perform this action in the spirit of Christ's love for God and neighbor?

To begin with, there are the obvious ecological considerations.

Modern construction methods are growing increasingly oblivious to the connection between housing and the materials that make up the house, and how they affect the occupants and the environment. Slapping together just any materials into a roof, walls, and floor does not automatically make a home. We wanted to avoid synthetics like Styrofoam, plastic, vinyl siding, plastic-based carpeting, plywood, and chemically treated lumber, all of which are harmful to people's health and the health of the ecosystems in which our homes are rooted.

We wished also to minimize the use of industrially produced products and rely instead on locally produced, renewable, low-tech, natural materials. We were partially successful in this. The commercial lumberyard in town was selling wood from British Columbia, thousands of miles away. So we bought most of our lumber from a local sawmill, the trees having been locally harvested. The straw bales were purchased from the wheat fields of nearby Quebec. We chose straw for the walls because it has great insulating abilities, so necessary in a cold climate such as we have in northern Vermont. The straw will last as long as it remains dry, yet will harmlessly return to the earth when the house finally finishes its life span.

We decided not to install electricity in the house. Water is provided at the kitchen sink by hand pump from a well dug ten feet deep. Lighting is by kerosene lamp and candles. The toilet is an outhouse one hundred feet out into the trees. We chose to attempt this low-tech life both to step outside of the maddening pace of modernity, and to reduce the burden that such a life places on others.

It has become increasingly clear to us over the years that, joined as we are to one another on the spiritual level, the excesses of modern life exact a price from our brothers and sisters. There is a reason that many people in the world struggle to have enough to eat. There is a reason that so many are crushed under an unendurable burden of poverty.

We who live the North American–Western European lifestyle would do well to ask ourselves what the connection is between how we live here and the immense suffering occurring in other parts of the world. If we see no connection, could it be that our way of life has desensitized us to the suffering of others? Is the high-tech, consumer lifestyle teaching us not to care for people and creation? Is our participation in the computer society making us an increasingly impersonal people?

To try to examine these questions, we've stepped outside the prevailing technology as far as we are able. Not having as many conveniences allows us to look at life from another angle. It enables us to get out from under some of the assumptions of the consumer society, and view life at a more essential level.

We start to become aware that water and food come from the earth. Wastes must be dealt with responsibly or they come back to poison us.

What exactly do we need to live meaningfully? The "one needful thing" in the spiritual life has its corollary in the physical life. Living simply teaches us that the physical and spiritual affect one another, that there is a deep connection between the two, that for the Christian the two are one. Knowing and experiencing this, perhaps we can find a way to live that eases the burden of the poor and strikes at the root causes of war.

Having been a carpenter for fifteen years, I found it pleasantly different to build a house without power tools. To be sure, it was more work. But it was work done in an atmosphere of loving fellowship. The quiet allowed us to be more mindful, in the manner of contemplative prayer. It gave us the opportunity to talk, to involve the children in aspects of the work they were able to do. Visitors who came to help seemed to appreciate the peacefulness of the work site.

I still use power tools in my carpentry work, because I am at present unable to earn a living otherwise. Perhaps eventually we can find another way to survive, but in any case our focus is not on achieving an elusive purity. Rather, we wish to move in a particular direction, seeking to be ever more faithful to the way of nonviolence and love taught and lived by our Lord. And to have as the foundation of our spiritual lives the love of God and neighbor.

It has been pointed out to us that one family living this way will not create any appreciable change. However, if we believe that all is connected on the spiritual level, then we do indeed affect and change one another. Each person's faithfulness is important, as witnessed by the biblical example of Noah's faithfulness, which saved the world from total destruction. And we know that the faithfulness of Christ is the pivotal accomplishment in history. Whatever our task, be it large or small, we wish to join that great tradition of attempting faithfulness.

In Praise of Human Power

CHUCK TRAPKUS

"This is how they used to make clothes long, long ago." The woman instructs her somewhat disinterested children, indicating me. I sit and spin my homegrown flax into linen and bite my tongue. "She's right, of course," I'm thinking. "But this is how I make clothes. Today." The notion that anyone would do this nowadays except as part of a folk arts-and-crafts festival like this one just does not compute with most people.

And then the smallest child notices my foot going up and down on the spinning wheel's treadle. "Look, Mommy," she cries. "His foot makes it go 'round!"

The little girl and I are both awestruck, she because she has encountered a human-powered machine—one of very few in her life save the bicycle and the Frisbee—and I because she is so amazed. A mere three or four generations ago the spinning wheel would have been nearly universally recognizable, and a few generations before that the flax processing I go around demonstrating would have been as commonplace as plastic wrap. As it is, that and so many other perfectly good, tried-and-true technologies have become quaint relics of bygone eras (a "bygone era" is the totality of human existence prior to about AD 1960).

The child's mother eventually remarks to other spectators, "It makes you wonder how they ever found the time to do all that." Today, if they think about it at all, most of our culture would ask, How did human beings manage to survive before electricity, the steam engine, and the internal combustion engine? How did they build houses, mow lawns, stay warm/cool, prepare food, watch TV?

I suspect we've all seen enough movies about the old days or so-called primitive societies to know some of the technical answers to that question: people used axes, looms, hand tools, forges, animals, windmills, waterwheels, etc. (While my focus in this article is human-powered technologies, I applaud and encourage the use of all low-tech alternatives such as harnessed animals, wind and water power, and passive solar power.)

But lest we in our ignorance make the same assumptions the woman made while watching me spin, let's be clear on one thing: Not everyone makes bread in an electric breadmaker. Not everyone has access to a phone. Not everyone has a refrigerator, a car, a toaster, a chainsaw. Billions of humans right now, sharing this same Mother Earth, get by with far fewer electric/atomic/petroleum-powered gadgets and appliances than we United States citizens. They may not all grind their own flour or weave their own cloth, but then, millions of them do. So when we ask how they ever did anything then, we should ask how they still do it now, and acknowledge our profound collective ignorance in so many basic matters of human sustenance.

An even better question would be, How and why did we ever cut ourselves off from the continuum of thousands of years of living by the work of our hands, of personal control over the means of our survival? How is it we know so little about using a scythe and so much about using a remote control? And yet we know so little about the aptly named remote control. We know only what GE or Panasonic wants us to know; they are in control.

Human beings not much different from you and me—except perhaps that they were a lot smarter when it came to providing for their own material needs—spun thread and wove it into fabric for thousands and thousands of years. And they still do so today, in places where the wicked plague of industrialization hasn't yet conquered them under the banners of progress, development, and global economy. What worked then still works now.

So the first reason I feel it's important to promote human-powered technologies is that they just make sense, and have done so practically since humanity's beginning. It does not make sense to me that the SaladShooter should make the ten-thousand-year-old knife and cutting board obsolete.

Secondly, they are superior to fossil-fuel technologies in that they are sustainable. Gas-powered cars will never last as long as, say, horse-powered ones, simply because there isn't enough fuel. And there's not enough nonrenewable fuel on earth for everyone to live as extravagantly, energywise, as the typical United States citizen does. Since everyone can't have it, why should only the rich? Whenever we live beyond the means of the rest of the planet's inhabitants, aren't we saying we're more important than they? These appliances exist to make our lives easier; the rest of the world be damned! Let's avoid it.

Thirdly, fossil fuel and nuclear technologies are notorious for contaminating our environment with pollutants and toxic wastes. Using the gas-powered blower/vac contributes to global warming; using a rake or push broom does not.

Fourthly, we are fast becoming a society of overweight, sedentary button pushers. Escalators and elevators are fine for those who physically can't use the stairs or for those who haul large loads; for the rest of us they're ridiculous. An electric can opener is helpful for an arthritic or one-armed person, absurd for most anyone else. And isn't it ironic that when we feel we aren't getting enough exercise from our computer-terminal, deep-fried-couch-potato-chip lifestyles, we can buy a membership at the Y and make some human-powered weights go perfunctorily up and down.

Still, many will argue that making our lives easier is what the car, the computer, and the electric toothbrush are all about. To them I ask, first, making whose life easier? Surely not the people who can't afford them. Not the generations who will have to reap the harvest of a polluted, wasted planet. And not the many who sweat away in inhumane factories for pennies a day to produce these short-lived marvels of modern obsolescence. Class chauvinism.

And second, are our lives really improved? With rare exceptions, our plug-'em-in, fill-'er-up technologies tend in the direction of making us dumber, lazier, more inactive, and less self-reliant.

Probably the best example of an accessible form of human power that can keep our bodies fit while significantly reducing air pollution is that of biking over car driving. Even in college towns where bikes are quite visible on the streets and in front of buildings, I can't help thinking that the bicycle is a vastly underrated means of transportation. A well-maintained bike is not only fast, quiet, cheap, clean, and easy to store compared to the car, but it is quite simply the most efficient way to get from point A to point B. Research done at Duke University in the '70s revealed that an adult on a ten-speed is the most efficient traveler there is, among birds, fish, insects, animals, planes, automobiles, etc. They calculated the amount of energy consumed per gram of body weight to travel one kilometer, for a variety of animals and machines. The bicyclist is nearly three times as efficient as the next in line, the salmon, and five times as efficient as walking. Cars are way back.

I use my bike for in-town commuting and some long-distance travel; I hope to do more and more. I use it only rarely for "recreational" trips, unless you believe as I do that anytime you're on a bike, it's recreation (except that one time I got us lost in the dark on winding, hilly, gravel roads near Sugar Creek last year). I use it to haul groceries, garden produce, my sons Isaac and Paul, bundles of newspapers, or whatever, in the trailer I built for it.

Some other human-powered technologies I make use of include:

1. Our ancient reel-type push mower. When it's sharp and adjusted properly, it's a great cutter and good exercise. It takes up less space in the garage, is lighter, safer, quieter, cheaper to purchase and use, and easier to maintain than a gas or electric version.

2. Our treadle sewing machine. I've used two other machines extensively, both electric, one with lots of fancy features, and there's no comparison. The simple, solidly built Singer my grandmother bought and used is a much better machine. While it lacks zigzag and backstitch capability, it will dependably plow right through multiple rolled seams of denim or doubled-up nylon webbing, handle rough or slippery fabrics and various threads without a slipped stitch and no need for tension adjustments. After many years of hard work and several years of neglect, it has never required more service than an occasional oiling.

3. My woodworking equipment. My foot-powered bow lathe is lightweight, is made mostly from softwoods, knocks apart, and will handle turnings up to about a foot in diameter and about four feet long. My bicycle-powered drill press is fast and efficient, not to mention fun to use. I do all sawing and planing by hand, and I've found that ripping long hardwood boards with a sharp, rip-tooth bow saw is a lot easier than I ever imagined when I was sold on electric table saws. A froe, hatchet, and drawknife make it possible for me to start with a log and have a wooden spoon in about an hour. Where nonelectric tools are not faster—sometimes they are—they are generally cheaper, easier to control, quieter, safer, easier to repair, and much longer lasting.

4. Our famous Underwood manual typewriter. The words you are reading were formed on it. I also make good use of a hand-crank food mill, oat roller, rotary shredder/grater, hand-generated flashlight, pocket abacus, cardboard fans, and a hand-powered guitar.

Certainly I make use of electricity and internal combustion engines from time to time as I feel it necessary. There can be a place
for them, especially as communally held appliances or devices for
physically handicapped persons. But we should use them sparingly
and consider well how best to get by as low on the technology chain
as possible.

It can be done; it is being done. Get that foot going!

Hand-Washing Your Clothes

BRENDA BAYLES

The thought of having to do laundry by hand strikes terror in the hearts of launderers everywhere. The list of insecurities is understandable: Will my clothes get clean? Isn't it a dreary chore? I haven't the time to do this!

But doing laundry by hand is neither dreary nor time-consuming after you've figured it out. And stains you once thought impossible to remove will begin to fade once you start washing manually!

Everyone should know how to hand-wash their clothes. To depend on any machine to take care of a basic need is foolhardy. Hand-washing is a skill that can be employed during camping trips, or just to do small articles between loads. It's perfect for washing cloth diapers (which, by the way, are the easiest articles to wash; jeans are the hardest!). And most importantly, the environmental impact is minimized by leaving out the electricity, and the water used can be run off to your garden to perform a second duty watering your veggies.

I wash an automatic-washer-size load in about ten minutes. Add five minutes for hanging it out on the clothesline and it's over. Really, it *is* this simple; the secret is to soak your clothing first.

The Basic Steps:

1. Fill two tubs with water, one for washing and one for rinsing.
2. Add bleach (or biodegradable hydrogen peroxide) and soap to the washtub if needed.

3. Let clothes soak according to manufacturer's instructions and how dirty they are.

4. Agitate each article separately by rubbing between your hands about five times.

5. Squeeze out excess water and throw article into the rinse tub.

Now that the washtub's empty and the rinse tub's full:

6. Swish the clothes a few times to rinse them.

7. Squeeze excess water out of the clothing and place it in a bucket.

8. Carry the bucket of clothes out and hang them up to dry.

You might want to sort your laundry before soaking it, just as you would for an automatic washer. This is a step I skip; I throw everything into the washtub and put the dark and delicate items on top. That way, I can wash and remove them first, then let everything else soak for another day.

Equipment

The only equipment required for hand-washing clothes is a five-gallon bucket and you. Soaking clothes eliminates the need for soap in most cases. If you have particularly oily or greasy clothes, you'll want to add some soap, usually right to the greasy spot, then soak. Most people use way too much soap; if you can smell it on your clothes, then it's still there, ready to irritate and cause allergies for the wearer. Plus, soap kills beneficial bacteria in the waterways it contaminates. A much more practical solution is to get the clothes clean, then hang them on the clothesline where fresh air and sunshine will make the clothes smell as clean as they are. And the beating of the clothes by the wind softens them; no one will ever guess that they didn't come out of a dryer.

Pieces that are being "freshened" rather than desoiled, such as sheets and bath towels, can be soaked, wrung, and hung up usually without a rinse if you leave out the soap. Unless the water looks like an inkwell, recycle it by using it to soak more items.

As a general rule, extremely soiled clothing should be soaked at least twenty-four hours. The minimum soak should be three hours, the exception being delicate articles. Laces, silks, and colors prone to running and fading should be washed after fifteen to thirty minutes of soaking. Use your judgment on how long to soak. In plain tepid water, with no soap and little or no bleach, it should be safe to soak for at least twenty-four hours on whites, less for bright colors and delicates.

Read clothes labels for clues. Your first few loads you'll want to check your clothes frequently to see how they—and the stains—are holding up. Personally, we are a farm family, and our clothes tend toward the indestructible, but my best clothes go on top of the load for a one-hour soak.

If an article is horribly stained or greasy, resort to soap or a commercial stain remover and rub it in well, then soak. As you load your washtub, be on the lookout for these problem areas and give them an extra five or so agitations before rinsing.

The only additive I use with any regularity is chlorine bleach. A mere capful or two will keep your wash water from smelling like it died, should you get busy and forget to wash for a couple of days. It also keeps diapers sanitary and white. Or use hydrogen peroxide.

Those old enameled double-rinse tubs with lids are the ideal setups for hand-washing. Beware of metal tubs that could leave rust stains on your garments.

One bucket instead of two will do; you'll simply have to empty out the used water, then refill it to rinse. And you'll have to set your washed clothes aside in the sink or on a clean, flat rock as you finish the load, then empty out the dirty water, refill the bucket with clean water, and toss the washed clothes in for a rinse. An extra bucket for rinsing lets you put the clothes right into the water so you don't have to move them an extra time.

Do use a solid bucket to carry the clothes outside, and not one of those el cheapo plastic woven things they have these days, or your laundry could drip on your shoes as you carry it to the clothesline.

Hot Water

I never use hot water for washing clothes. Soaking replaces the need for it, and hot water is heated with a natural resource, be that coal, wood, or electricity. Save those resources for cooking and bathing, and let soaking battle your stains for you. There will be less chance of shrinkage, fading, or other damage to your clothes if you leave out the assault of hot water.

Washboards

Too much work. Will also leave you open to "grandma" jokes from your spouse. Hand agitating puts the article in both of your hands and in your control; rub a stain against another portion of the article, or a washcloth for more abrasiveness, and it will be just as clean as a clumsy washboard will get it.

Wringers

Forget 'em. Wringers break buttons and zippers, take up your time, and work you to death. A quick squeeze or wring is all that's necessary before moving on to the next article of clothing. Don't waste your time trying to wring out every last drop; a little extra "drip" in your clothes won't hurt a thing; the sun will take care of those for you.

Clothes in rinse water just need to be swished a few times, then wrung out and put in a bucket to transport them to the clothesline. Again spare yourself and don't try to squeeze out every droplet of water. Automatic washers must do that, or a clothes dryer would never get them dried out. But my personal dryers, the sun and the wind, are quite versatile and will dry, fluff, and perfume my clothes perfectly, without costing me or the environment a dime.

One last lecture about hand-washing clothes: insist on familial participation in this event. Your spouse can haul water if you aren't washing near a spigot, the kids can hang the clothes out and bring in dry ones, and everyone can carry their dirty clothes to the soaking tub and their clean, dry clothes to their rooms. You will be richly rewarded with clean clothes, a clean environment, and a family that knows the joy of shared responsibilities.

Unplugging the Media

A story that appeared a number of years ago in the Amish publication Family Life *told of a busload of tourists who visited an Amish farmer. The group consisted of people from many religious denominations. One of them said, "We already know all about Jesus Christ, but what does it mean to be Amish?" The Amish fellow thought for a moment, and then asked for a show of hands for how many in the tour group had televisions. Every hand went up. Then he asked how many thought that maybe having a television contributed to a lot of social and spiritual problems in society. Again, every hand went up. In light of this, he asked, how many would be willing to give up having television. This time, no hands went up. He went on to explain that this was the essence of being Amish: a willingness to do without something if that thing is not good for them spiritually.*

People and communities can choose which technologies to accept or reject. Our essayists claim spiritual and moral bases for accepting or rejecting media. They represent a spectrum, decisions made by people moving in pretty much the same direction, away from the virtual and toward the real. As you read their words, you can't fail to note the many instances where they apply specific criteria to explain their paths. However invested in modern media you may be at present, surely some of their questioning will be useful to you as you seek authentic communication, not just media saturation.

Mix and Match

James Huskins

Our buggy is not just a hobby; we drive the horse for transportation. No one requires us to do so. We make the choice, and we make it joyfully, but that choice must color the way I see other options. No doubt the buggy affects my sense of what is appropriate.

For instance, the mention of some combinations offends me. Honey and catsup; rap and Mozart; a 300-horsepower tractor in a small garden; the comedy team of Groucho Marx and Dan Quayle—these associations at least smack of the offensive. The idea of repugnant combinations plagues me lately because of the suspicion that I might have created one. I'm afraid I have fostered an offensive pairing of technologies.

Tools and books are my material weaknesses. Each time we move I kick myself for not taking up stamp collecting instead, but tools and the knowledge to use them well excite me. For thirty years I have spent countless hours thinking about the kinds of tools I need, which brands to buy, how to maintain and store them, and above all, how to make the best use of them.

For most of that time my guiding principle has been whether these tools are "appropriate." Appropriateness means more than whether a tool is well made, well suited to the job at hand, not likely to break down in use, and has a long life expectancy, although all these factors are part of the equation.

Also involved are questions such as: Does the manufacture

and/or use of this tool seriously degrade the environment? Does owning this tool make me more or less dependent on corporations whose scruples are as readily for sale as their products? Does the use of this tool enhance my ability to think well and my capacity to provide for basic needs? Is the tool obscenely expensive to purchase and/or use? Will the kingdom of God be any closer to existing on earth as it is in heaven if I have this tool?

Together, these questions cover a lot of ground, and they have affected the major directions of my life.

For example, my decision to purchase and use a horse and buggy grew out of applying these criteria to the automobile. We still have a car, but the buggy is more appropriate. The buggy does everything well except cover great distance at the speed to which we have become addicted. Addiction to speed cannot be a good thing, but that thought brings up the paradox—the possibly offensive combination of technologies—that I have created.

Long after many of my friends and associates computerized their lives, I steadfastly resisted adoption of such complex and expensive technology.

Personal computers seemed inappropriate in many ways. Furthermore, I saw wholesale abdication of the ability to think and act autonomously by people who had become computer dependent. It's not enough that no one can do simple math without a calculator. We now have cashiers who cannot make change, librarians who cannot find books on the shelves, sales clerks who cannot write a bill of sale, secretaries who cannot use an appointment book; the list goes on. Seeing this happen in the early '80s frightened me to the point that I vowed never to turn over my thinking to anyone or anything. That vow, coupled with prevalent high prices, made it easy for me to resist the personal computer revolution—at least for a while.

During my first pastorate, after eleven years in the business world, I did all sermon composition and other writing the old-fashioned way.

This worked fine, but I noticed that as my sermon style matured, the amount of time I spent putting it all together became oppressive. Since many of my parishioners expected me to spend every waking moment on church work, this arrangement worked well enough, but I could not avoid the suspicion that I was doing something the wrong way. The issue came to a head when we moved to a larger church.

Resting innocently on my new desk was a small package that changed my life. It was a word processor/typewriter—crude by computer standards, but a quantum leap away from my ballpoint. I don't recall struggling very much before opening the instruction manual. From that moment it became nearly impossible for me to commit longhand. My life was as radically altered as that of the first Native American who received a steel sheath knife from some European explorer. The stone-age tools would no longer cut it.

The object of my addiction stayed behind when we left that church for a brief fling with a research institute, but it didn't matter because my new employer had computers galore. I always had ready access. The symptoms of true addiction did not surface until we left that job for another pastorate, and I found myself back in the business of producing a sermon every week with pen and notepad. Longhand seemed to take even longer now, and the mechanics were more oppressive. It didn't take long for me to convince myself that the Huskins family needed a computer.

We ended up with a PowerBook. That's a Macintosh portable about the size of my Bible concordance and several times more capable than the desktop computer at my last job. It seems to do everything well, and I am convinced that it saves five to ten hours a week in sermon preparation alone. What's more, in a display of true addiction, I now use the computer on the pulpit and scroll through my notes on the screen. This system works well and will, over time, save a lot of paper and landfill space. Even though the computer system was a huge investment for us, I am convinced it was money well spent.

Why, then, am I still so uncertain about owning the thing at all?

Here I come back to the questions. This marvelous gray machine *did* cost a lot of money. It *does* make me dependent on corporations that operate outside my definition of morality. It *does* contain the potential for serious impairment of my already limited ability to think. Most damning of all, I fear that the use of a computer embodies the possibility of becoming even more dependent on human cleverness and less so on the God who made heaven and earth. No matter which way I turn this issue, I do not find satisfaction.

For now I am content to call a truce with myself on the subject. We have the machine, and I will continue to use it, but not without some nagging doubt. I intend to nurture that doubt. I also intend to pray for wisdom and humility in the face of the incredible power of my PowerBook.

On the other hand, our computer frees up time for buggy driving. That's when I seem to do my best thinking and reconnecting with life and God and my calling. I realize that many will see it as a paradox that I use time saved by a computer to travel slower, but I suppose those are the same ones who may be offended by the eerie, green glow that can sometimes now be see through the buggy window.

A Drive to Consume

Franklin Saige

A few days ago I was shopping inside a retail warehouse the size of an airplane hangar. This one was devoted to graphic supplies, and I was trying to track down some special printer's ink. After a bit of looking and not finding, and several visits to the computer terminal to check inventory, the salesperson indicated we would need to consult with someone in the front office. I was led through a door and into a series of hallways leading to a vast, low-ceilinged room crowded with partitioned cubicles.

The air in this place virtually hummed with electricity from the bright lights. I smelled ozone and off-gassing polymer resin. Glancing about I saw that almost every object, every hard surface and textile in sight, was made from plastic. My guide and I were looking for "Debbie." As we searched, he stood on tiptoe and peeked over the wall of every cubicle, whispering, "Debbie? Debbie?"

We never found Debbie, although we greeted many of her colleagues at work in their boxes. They generally seemed not unhappy to be there, pulling themselves away from computer screens to say hello. Pale, perhaps, and slightly lethargic, but seemingly content. And, of course, there was the novelty of meeting me, a plain person dressed in clothing more common to the eighteenth century than the twentieth. That probably doesn't happen every day in their office. I know that being in such a place isn't an everyday occurrence for me.

The combination of so many people and computers confined in that room reminded me of a prominent bit of poetry I saw in newspapers and magazines a few years ago. I suppose it was recited on television as well. The title was "What Is Newton?" and the first verse went:

Newton is digital.
Newton is personal.
Newton is as powerful as a computer.
Newton is as simple as a piece of paper.
Newton is a new kind of technology.

Another verse:

Newton will help you get organized.
Newton can help you make phone calls.
Newton can help manage your schedule.
Newton can help you plan your day.
Newton is always looking for ways to help you out.

The final couplet:

Newton is here today.
Newton will be everywhere tomorrow.

We are living in a time when the delivery of advertising poetry is instantaneous and ubiquitous. Newton, as you surely know, is a MessagePad computer, and the poem was an ad. I like the Newton poem in particular because it so brashly proclaimed to the millions who work in situations such as the graphic-supply warehouse that a more advanced computer was going to make their work *even easier* and their lives *even better*.

Surely this must be a winning argument, or it wouldn't be used so frequently. We've come a long way: Newton and Apple Computer have been rescued by Bill Gates. Microsoft and every other technology product propagandize us over and over through television advertising. And yet, anyone who steps back even slightly from their promises can see that work and life have speeded up and become more difficult and less enjoyable—or at least less experiential—since computer and video technology have come of age.

Perhaps the creators of the Newton were slightly uncertain that their enthusiasm would go over (the MessagePad never did catch on), because they backed it up with a little rhetorical threat: the Newton would "be everywhere tomorrow"—including your cubicle—

whether you like it or not. And it's true, at least in the larger sense; high technology is now in place everywhere it isn't needed, from the local pizza parlor (where it takes a lot longer to place an order over the telephone due to the needs of screen and keyboard) to the church newsletter.

Following the Newton ode to a new machine, the first mercantile rejoicings over the coming "information superhighway" have arrived, and they, too, invoke art to sell change. They began with a televised ad for MCI that reportedly featured a child star chanting, "There will be a road. It will not connect two points. It will connect all points. . . . It will not go from here to there. There will be no there, there. We will all only be here."

Maybe this was actually a profound utterance, rather than the baloney it appeared to be, if we listen more carefully. As the rumble of the bulldozers clearing the way for the information superhighway gets louder, it's time to listen, and ask ourselves just where exactly is this "Here" where we will all be?

The explicit goal of the electronics revolution that brings us such wonders as the Newton is to turn machines into people—people of a lowly station to be sure, but intelligent and understanding servants nevertheless.

But it is obvious to those who choose to remain outside this revolution that personal computers, networks, video entertainment, and television—in short, all the technological components now coalescing into the information superhighway—are turning people into machines. If that seems too strong, allow me to go even further and say that perhaps we are *actually being put inside the machine*. Maybe that's where the Here is, inside a world run by the laws of Newton.

Computers first invaded work and leisure when their hitherto mysterious operation could be presented as something users already understood. Apple popularized the desktop metaphor and a what-you-see-is-what-you-get video-screen representation that makes it easy to use computers to organize and carry out work. The selling of this technology originally took the form of promising that the personal computer would revolutionize work by decentralizing it. And we would become a paperless society to boot. The advertising campaign introducing the Apple Macintosh had the theme of lone rebellion toppling the System.

I have noticed that left-wing activists and environmentalists have taken this message to heart and joined the multimedia revolution with a vengeance. For them, decentralization and mobilization are attractive technological promises.

Walking through the warren of cubicles at the graphic-supply warehouse, however, I realized once again that we haven't really mastered the computer's metaphor of friendly desktop liberator. Instead, the metaphor has made it possible for us to be drawn by stages into the machine's reality. A better metaphor might be the fairy tale of Hansel and Gretel. Like the two lost children, we happily approach the metaphor of the gingerbread house, only to find that inside lies a prison. At present, Microsoft is the warden.

Outside the house that Bill built is "reality," which is not a metaphor for anything. Reality, for those few of us who are not yet Here in the world of the information superhighway, consists of life. Despite the godlike pretensions of our culture, all of us actually are still connected to the whole of life—complex, changing, open-ended, yet intimately connected, a cyclic coming-to-be and passing away. Furthermore, this real-life stuff is not controlled by us or our ideas, wishes, or commands. Those who live in the Mississippi floodplain or on the San Andreas Fault already know this.

We *all* know it on some level, but that hasn't stopped very many from trying to wrest control of the creation from the Creator. The discovery in the last century of oil and its use as energy resource and material feedstock has convinced our society that we have the power to depart from the natural cycle and bulldoze a path to total control of ourselves and the environment. To fully conquer our natural dependence on the real world, this path must now become a broad road, a superhighway leading humanity to the place where everywhere is Here.

And there is no moral restraint in creating this road. That is, unfortunately, one of the perils of modern technology: it is invented to be sold, as opposed to most earlier inventions, which were made to be used by the community, the inventor himself, or his patron. Modern technology comes clothed in seductive images of freedom in order to make the sale, but it can take away our freedom once we buy into it. It takes away our freedom by reducing our ability to choose—for example, our ability to choose not to think in terms of organization or having our schedules "managed." It takes away our freedom by narrowing our options to a set of preprogrammed choices. Its screen-based nature removes the sensory complexity that is the most obvious characteristic of the lived world. We are discovering that sitting in front of a screen all day is hardly the same thing as overthrowing Big Brother.

Most people still believe technology barely influences how we live our lives. "It's what we *do* with technology that counts," they tell me. It all strictly depends upon our moral fitness, our will to master the machine.

I suppose even the most seductive forms of technology can be resisted, at least for a while. For example, people resisted using automobiles at first. Many people thought the automobile would be too noisy, too fast, too haughty, and just plain too expensive to fit the existing social fabric. Initially, most people did not buy one. However, even though their fears (and worse) about the automobile were quickly realized, soon everyone who could afford to own one, did. Then these automobiles were used in ways that gradually led to the weakening of the family and the community, and the destruction of the landscape.

If hundreds of millions of car owners could ostensibly choose how they would use this technology, what happened to make them choose destructive rather than supportive uses? Did they simply change their values on a whim? Or did something inherent in the technology pull them in a particular direction?

What does the automobile do *best*: pull families apart, cause urban sprawl, distort our sense of distance, or make travel more convenient and speedy?

If we likewise want to know where the information super-highway is leading us, maybe we should ask ourselves what *it* will do *best*.

To follow this road, we need to know that the term *information superhighway* is, like the Newton poem, strictly the creation of the advertising muse. It was coined to piggyback on the prestige of the information highway of interactive (meaning *two-way*) networked computers sharing text and data known as the Internet. What makes the superhighway super is that it will be a commercially run interactive video- and Internet-based network put together by the mega tele-communication, software, and cable television industries. *Interactive Pay-TV* would be a more accurate name for it, though the Internet and similar data networks form the infrastructure. A truer definition of the information superhighway would focus on its somewhat less lofty pursuits: video shopping, pay-per-view movies on demand (presently a $10 billion annual market for video rental stores), and two-way videophones. And don't forget Web sites for everyone, in-cluding the family dog. Now everyone can be heard, howling into the network along with . . . everyone else.

Once the billions of dollars to build the system have been spent, everywhere will be Here. More precisely, every marketer will be Here—in the living room and inside heads—because entertainment viewing choices, and especially video and Internet shopping buying preferences, are monitored and analyzed, so that advertisers can turn around and market to you in a very targeted manner. Imagine one day using your television to purchase cloth diapers over the Internet from the virtual Wal-Mart. Right after that, you switch to an entertainment program and voilà! The commercials are all for Pampers, piped to your specific household as a result of your latest purchasing profile. That is, at any rate, the commercial dream, very interactive in its own way, though not exactly in the poetic way it is being portrayed. And it could be even worse than I have painted it, because personal communication (videophones, E-mail) and all other text and data entering the superhighway would in theory be available for analysis to the same end.

Whatever the specific route the superhighway finally takes, it is obviously going to be *best* at marketing more goods and services. It will be *best* at invading your private life. Ultimately, its *best* use will be in driving up consumption, something that appeals to marketers somewhat more than to me, concerned as I am about the condition of the planet and my soul. I don't know about you, but I need less temptation to buy things, not more. And I don't want to be constantly sold to.

Jerry Mander's book *In the Absence of the Sacred* lists "Ten Recommended Attitudes about Technology." Along with number one ("Since most of what we are told about new technology comes from its proponents, be deeply skeptical of all claims") and number two ("Assume all technology 'guilty until proven innocent' "), my favorite is number five: "Never judge a technology by the way it benefits you personally. Seek a holistic view of its impacts. The operative question is not whether it benefits you, but who benefits most? And to what end?"

I try to keep these criteria in mind when someone suggests that because some particular need of theirs is being met by a computer or television or interactive network, these technologies can be used "for good, too. It just depends on what we do with them." Since people appear to be more enslaved in their work and home lives than ever before, we could instead ask ourselves whether the problems computers and electronic media seem to alleviate can be traced to the advent of computers themselves. Haven't computers and television speeded up economic life and increased social chaos?

The fact is, these technologies wouldn't exist if not for their utility as pillars of the consuming society.

To use an example from the real superhighway, take the emergency response vehicle called an ambulance. An ambulance is perceived as a "good" use for the internal combustion engine. It can take people from a car wreck to the hospital in minutes. But it takes a whole society of energy-guzzling car buyers addicted to mobility and speed to provide the marketing momentum for automobiles, including ambulances, to be produced. And this "good" ambulance would hardly be needed in the absence of its patron technology, the crash-prone automobile.

We are presently being assured that stepping into the virtual reality of the information superhighway and opening our minds to it is also a good thing. Doubtless there will be many examples of this good: Grandma will be able to see the grandkids on the videophone. The disabled will have more opportunities for inclusion.

And we will hear more and more about "virtual communities"— an exciting concept because, after all, the real ones have pretty much disappeared.

Perhaps almost-real ones will suffice for you, but not for me. I am unwilling to accept being part of a technology that can exist only if it drives me to consume more, in a process that drains my will to seek out real community.

A woman at an organic farming conference I attended last winter told the program speaker, who was against most high technology, that even though she, too, thought these technologies might be harmful, still she felt she had to keep up with them. "Since this is what's going on in the world, don't we have to participate, just to survive?" No one could answer her then, and I have only part of the answer myself.

I can say only that I'm unwilling to drive the superhighway into the land of Here, and I know that many others are at the point of having to decide whether to continue on this ride or find an exit. On the other hand, the people I glimpse in their cubicles, or sitting around their TV hearths at home, don't yet seem too dissatisfied. What will wake them up? How can I help them reverse direction and get back out of the machine?

I have no interest in being part of a movement to ban or boycott. To do that, I would have to become like my friends in the ecology movement, *connected* to computer networks in order to *exchange information* and get *organized*. I see the technology encouraging in them precisely the way of relating to lived experience that has brought about the crises they seek to alleviate.

My strategy for exiting the information superhighway is simply never to enter it. The only direct action I can take is to live a real life, in real time, without viewing or networking or overconsuming anything. No input, no output.

And I am going to tell anyone who will listen that the Here of real life, in real community, in real reality, is better than the virtual Here of the information superhighway any day of the week. That real and virtual are in fact speeding along in entirely opposite directions.

Why the Amish Can Live without Television

DAVID WAGLER

There are millions of people in this world who do not watch television. Not because they have any objection to it, but because it is not economically feasible for them to do so. But here in the U.S. almost anyone who wants to watch television, can. Even convicts in their prison cells have the opportunity.

The average person in this country spends more than three hours daily in front of the television set. It is now the third most time-consuming activity after working and sleeping.

Sometimes I think it would be interesting to have access to television. News comes on at different times of the day, as well as the market reports, and in the evening the weather. I have always been an avid weather observer and to me it would be interesting to know what the weather conditions are over the country at the moment. The jet stream is a subject that has always intrigued me, as often it is directly overhead.

The weather maps in the newspapers do not show the jet stream. However, on television I understand the weatherman points it out every evening. He also shows what effect it may be having on our weather for the next few days. There is no other way this information is available to me, but if I had a television set, it would be there for the viewing—provided I were willing to pay the price.

Moneywise, the cost is not all that great. Everyone knows that broadcast television (as opposed to cable) is free. All you need to do is buy a set to capture the electromagnetic waves and bring them into your living room. The advertisers pay for the rest. Or do they?

What about the hidden costs?

So you didn't know there were any hidden costs?

As far back in history as we can go, the family unit has been the basis of civilization. The first four of the Ten Commandments have to do with our relationship to God. The last five Commandments outline our dealings with man and are the basis for law the world over. The Fifth Commandment, the center and axis of our relationship with both God and man, has to do with the family. Without a strong family unit, all other institutions fail.

This Commandment sets up the family unit in a way that is sustainable. Children are to honor and obey their parents. This theme goes all the way through the Bible, and no one has yet found a successful substitute for it. Parents are responsible for the welfare of their children. The only way in which they can fulfill this mandate is to exercise their authority to train them in the way they should go.

During World War II, Adolf Hitler decided it was the business of the German state to raise the children. He considered his nation to be a superior race of people destined to rule the world. To further this aim, he urged unwed women to give birth to children fathered by brave soldiers. These children were to be raised by the state to become the citizenry of the most powerful nation in the world.

Shortly after World War II another powerful influence appeared that also threatened to disrupt the family unit, but in a more subtle way. It was called television and it brought into the home what had formerly been seen only in theaters. At first there was an outcry from those concerned with the possible effects of the undertaking, but this soon died down. The flaunting of a TV antenna over the top of the home shortly came to be a symbol of affluence. People who would not have allowed their children to go to the theater now allowed this latest idol into their homes.

By 1950, city dwellers, as well as many who lived in rural areas, had pretty well accepted this innovation. This was the year our family moved into a county that might have been classed as underdeveloped. Much of the housing was at poverty level. The truck drivers who moved us into our new home took back the report that the county did not have television. We soon found this was not true. In driving through the countryside we found homes that were little more than shacks, but they did have TV antennae waving over them. It was a matter of only a few years before they were commonplace. Nothing could impede the advance of progress!

The coming of television brought along with it an entirely new dimension to the home. Now children spent a lot of time in front of the television set, as well as selecting what they wanted to see. At first there was not much choice as to which station or type of program they could watch. When the advertisers discovered what it was the viewers wanted, they began to cater to the demand, and usually at the lowest denominator. Moral standards were quickly on the downgrade. The majority of the programs were nothing more than pure entertainment with a constantly deteriorating moral climate.

Among our people, we often have friends or relatives coming to visit us from other communities. If it is someone we think a lot of, we sometimes call a meeting to visit with them or make use of their talent. Could you imagine that if, for example, a current rock star had come to our house, we would have called our neighbors together to see and hear him?

Having TV in the home is the same as allowing such entertainers to perform inside our homes. We consider it important that our children grow up in an environment that exposes them as little as possible to the temptations of this world. We even try to shield them from reading harmful books.

Our children are taught to accept the Bible at face value and follow its teachings. To "do your own thing" is foolish and self-destructive. We were brought up to believe that the family is the foundation of the nation and that marital infidelity and divorce lead to the breakdown of the family. It is an indisputable fact that the rapid decline in moral values, which is even today continuing, coincided with the coming and growth of television. Many feel there must be a direct connection of cause and effect.

When we as parents bring a television into our home, we are abdicating our position as head of the family. This is tantamount to surrendering our responsibility of training our children. We are inviting the values of Hollywood and New York into our living room. We are turning over the key to our home and our hearts to the world. When the world is invited into our homes, it accepts the invitation and proceeds to take over. It will claim the thinking and mental outlook of ourselves and all others in the family. This monster will demand complete submission to its own set of values. We can delay the action by putting restrictions on what we watch or what our children are allowed to see, but it will only slow the pace leading to the ultimate destination.

Our people, the Amish, have taken our stand and refuse to bow to this god of TV. We choose to continue to try to fulfill the God-given responsibility of being the head of our own home. We believe it is our duty to provide a wholesome atmosphere for ourselves and our children.

We admit it would be convenient to have television sets in our homes to get the news, the markets, and the weather report. But we don't think we can afford it. The price is too high. We would sooner sacrifice our convenience in order to make more effective our efforts in raising our children. We don't think it is fair to ourselves or our children to be constantly exposed to the example and teachings of those who do not have the knowledge of the true God. We will not invite the false gods that personify the goals of this world to enter our homes. That is the reason we do not submit to having television.

The Media-Free Family

MARY ANN LIESER

My husband and I have lived without television for a long time—the four years of our marriage plus at least five prior years, separately, for each of us. It has been more recently that we've given up radio, as well. For over a year now we've lived without voices in our home save those of the real, live people who live here or those of visiting friends.

We talked about it for a long time. I believed ridding our home of radio would be a positive move for us, individually and as a family. And I also resisted the idea. I listened to several hours of public radio news broadcasting morning and evening, and I was reluctant to give that up. "Later," I said. It was autumn of an election year, and I wanted to listen to the presidential candidates debate. We put it off time and again. Then one morning over breakfast we decided to drop off at Goodwill that day all the radios we owned. And so we did it.

I felt light and free, as I always do when I give away things I no longer need, clearing out a little more space in my life and my home. I also felt as if I were at sea. How would I know what was going on in the world? How would I keep up with things and stay connected? Those questions—of such importance to me then—seem almost silly now, but it's been a long journey to get from there to here.

A week passed before I stopped reaching for the radio in the kitchen each morning to listen to the news before I even started breakfast. The next thing I noticed was how oppressive silence can be. When our daughter was learning to talk, shortly before we gave our radios away, she would point at the radio that sat on our kitchen counter and say, "Guy talking." When she noticed it was gone and pointed to the empty space it used to occupy, I told her, "No more guy talking. It's just us talking now," and I wondered how we would fill up all that space of silence that used to be filled with voices from the airwaves.

With nothing to fill the silence but my own voice, I began singing. I had been singing to my almost-two-year-old daughter since her birth, but only a song here or there. I would quickly run through all the songs I knew the words to, and then find myself struggling to remember some more. What were those ones we sang around the campfire in sixth grade? How did the second verse of "Go Tell Aunt Rhody" go? I sought out songbooks at our local library and relearned dozens of songs from my childhood, songs that I'd not sung in years, and it was fun. We've learned many new songs together, too, ones I'd never known before. Hymns and songs of praise, old folk tunes, lullabies, silly songs, sentimental ballads— our heritage in music.

I am not a good singer. My husband still winces sometimes when I switch keys in the middle of a melody, but he would be the first to say that my ability to carry a tune has improved a hundred-fold. Best of all, I discovered that I love to sing. I sing unselfconsciously all day long and so does my now three-year-old daughter: "Clementine" as we do the breakfast dishes, "Greensleeves" to the baby as I rock him, "Riding in the Buggy, Miss Mary Jane" as we sweep, "Down in the Valley" as we tidy up the living room, "Old Dan Tucker" as I hang the wash out on the line, "Joyful, Joyful, We Adore Thee" as we set off on a walk.

Human voice fills our house and is richer than any electronically generated sound could be. My children, now ages one and three, live in a world that is full of music, and they have learned by example that singing is something real people can do for the pure joy of it, not as something we pay entertainers to do for us. And they have learned that it is definitely not something you have to be very good at to feel worthy of doing.

Everyone is worthy of the joy that can come with a spontaneous song, but many people who have electronically generated voices as a constant presence with which to compare themselves, believe they should possess perfect pitch and a backup orchestra to be worthy of singing. We don't compare ourselves to anything, except maybe the silence, and to us our voices are more beautiful than anything that ever came into our home over the airwaves.

We don't sing or talk all the time, though. The silence that I was always compelled to fill up has become beautiful to me, as well. I've become accustomed to being quiet with my own thoughts, and now—especially when I do chores such as washing the dishes—I can be centered and meditative in a way I never could be when I either was listening to talk radio or had voices from it still echoing in my head. This calm and centered way of being in my daily life fits better with the slower pace toward which my family is striving.

Radio has become like so many other things we've given up, or made a conscious decision to live without, from television to a clothes dryer. Our lives have become much richer, in more ways than we could have imagined when we were living with what we have since given up, whether it be a convenience, a luxury, or a laborsaving device.

Although I don't have the freedom to listen that I had with a radio—freedom to hear over a dozen stations at any hour of the day or night—I have a different and more fulfilling freedom: freedom from having radio voices and noises in my house and in my head. And, of course, I'm free of the compulsion to turn the radio on to alter my mood or distract myself from my own thoughts. Often when I had a radio I would feel compelled to listen to the news even when I didn't really want to, just to make sure I wasn't missing anything. Now that the choice is removed, I have much more freedom to choose when I want to learn about the news of the day.

And what about "missing" things? How do I keep up and stay connected? How do I know what's going on in the world? Now that I've lived this way for over a year, I can safely conclude that those questions that were of such concern to me really aren't issues at all. The news—developments in world or local events—is always there, and I often have a better and deeper understanding of such events when I can spend concentrated and focused time once a week reading about them. I can scan reading material and decide how much time I want to spend reading about any given topic. I have the power to decide, rather than letting National Public Radio choose how much of my mental time will be devoted to Bosnia and how much to Somalia.

Not having a radio actually means I'm better informed about world and local events. Not having a radio means I can better focus my attention on my children playing in the room while I make supper; thus I'm better attuned to their needs and moods. Not having a radio means I have more control over what fills my mind, and it means I'm more comfortable with and accepting of silence. Not having a radio means I've learned more about silence, about the many kinds and textures of quietness that can fill a house. Ultimately, not having a radio means for me that I am more fully human, more involved in forming my own mental landscape and in relating to the other people in my life.

And I can't help but believe that my children are growing up with a much richer childhood for not having electronic media in our home. They, too, are learning about the textures of quietness. And, of course, they are doing what children are best at: learning to fill up the silence in their own way. Right now my daughter is making up her own verses to "Here We Go Round the Mulberry Bush" and singing them to her doll, and my son, though he doesn't yet talk, is babbling the tune to "Skip to My Lou" on key.

Reclaiming Distance and Place

David Wagler, in his weekly letter appearing in The Budget *and* Der Botschaft *Amish newspapers, once noted that people who admire the Amish and want to emulate their ways sometimes make the mistake of thinking it is what the Amish* do *that makes them who they are. David pointed out that it is instead* who they are, *as Christians, that dictates Amish choices in how to live. As each of us tries to live according to our beliefs, however, the daily choices we make will ultimately either strengthen or undermine our spiritual growth.*

As plain people, we find ourselves and our communities striving to choose social relationships and material artifacts that support our beliefs. Regrettably, for conservative Friends (Quaker) such as Mary Ann and I, this means pretty much starting from scratch, since our communities and our culture of plainness are just beginning to revive after decades of disintegration. The task is made doubly hard for those raised in the modern world who wish to join plain communities. Cultural assumptions and even your rationality will be tested by the stringent views and practices of communities that view the Bible as a blueprint for living.

If such constancy stops you short, so be it. As the essays in this section prove, for every model of community, there exists an alternative. Where we cannot agree, we can at least be persuaded of the seriousness and goodwill of those who have not only made the commitment to doing things differently, but have committed themselves to their brothers and sisters.

The Cart before the Horse

SETH HINSHAW

Every Fourth Day,* I look through my county's weekly paper. It is a strange habit. Our paper decided several years ago not to carry any state or national news, and as a result, practically all of the articles concern people from around the county, most of whom I don't know.

So my major interest in the paper is not to learn all the latest crime news; I look at some headlines and then read through the classified ads to see what's for sale. I usually am finished within five minutes.

There are rarely any classifieds that are directed toward plain Friends such as myself—like "'Lots of old Quaker books," or "Need information on George Fox and John Wilbur." One week, though, there was an interesting classified ad that caught my attention. A farmer not far from where I lived listed several items he was selling. In the middle of the list was "an old Dunkard buggy."

It was exciting to see a buggy listed, so I told my friend Susie about it. We discussed the ad, and throughout our conversation, two important questions kept resurfacing. The first concerned the value of the buggy. I knew absolutely nothing about horses or buggies. What if I spent a lot of money for something that ended up being too expensive to repair? What was a pristine buggy worth? The value question, while important, was easily solved. We went to visit

---

*Conservative Friends (Quakers) do not use the common names of days and
  months, substituting numbers. Fourth Day is Wednesday.

one of Susie's Amish neighbors, and he agreed to go with us to look over the buggy.

Answering the second question was much more difficult; why in the world would anyone desire to own a buggy? One could, I suppose, counter with the rhetorical question, Why would anyone want to own a television? And since Friends in general are often portrayed as antiquarians or an experiment in living history, it is easy to incorporate a horse and buggy into the stereotype. After all, William Penn rode in buggies.

These responses, however, avoid the question of why we, as plain Friends, might want to use a horse and buggy for our primary mode of transportation. Historically speaking, most Friends communities had broken up before the invention of the automobile, and in many places we were among the first to own cars. A few Friends continued to buck the trend toward automobiles through World War II. Proof that some Friends felt unhappy with the transition to automobiles is found in two families in eastern Ohio, both of which claim to be the last Friends to set aside the horse.

The more I thought on the second question, the more I came to realize that our choice of transportation has a big effect on our lifestyle. Deciding to make a transportation change would change practically all the other areas of my life. At present, for example, if I want ice cream, I can drive into town and get it. Then later in the same day I can go back to town if I want to go to the library. If I relied on horse-powered buggy transportation, it wouldn't be possible to make such spur-of-the-moment decisions. Trips into town would likely become semiweekly and involve doing all of my trading in one visit. Anything I forgot would just have to wait, so hopefully I would be more careful to write down everything I needed.

More importantly, there would be fewer occupational choices. Right now I drive forty minutes to work. A horse would take at least several hours to make the same journey. So making the switch would force me to live near my work. As a result, I would probably go out of the printing business and either farm or open a small, locally oriented business. Either option would promote the local economy.

The financial objections to horse-drawn transportation are mostly superficial, I think. Automobiles are, after all, expensive. I usually spend enough money on automobile upkeep and gas each year to buy and board several teams of horses. And, of course, there are the related expenses of insurance, licenses, etc. So I could work locally on a farm, earning thousands of dollars less than at my faraway job, and actually have more money to spend if I drove a horse instead of a car.

Another major consideration in trying to answer the question of why to go back to the horse is the issue of stewardship of the earth. Because the earth is the Lord's, and the fullness thereof, we will be answering some tough questions one day for wasting and polluting the creation. We all know that the internal combustion engine is a primary source of pollution and has greatly contributed to the greenhouse effect, which may bring about global warming. And do we *really* need trucking companies to deliver six-day-old produce to local grocery stores? Why can't a local farmer grow the produce for the grocery store and keep the money in local hands?

To sum it all up, a move to horse transportation would be a move toward stronger communities and less dependence on inputs of energy and material from somewhere else. These answers convinced me.

When the fateful day arrived, Susie and I drove to pick up Warren (her Amish neighbor) to go have a look at the buggy. On the way to the farm, I asked Warren some questions about the price. He pointed out that since Dunkard buggy regulations were so different from Amish specifications, no Amish would be interested. That would help keep the price down. But he would have to see the buggy before saying what he would pay for it.

The owner of the buggy even had a neat story of his own. He was going to buy a farm near town and decided to buy a buggy because of the lower cost compared to driving a car. So he bought a buggy from a

German Brethren—a Dunkard—living near Plain City. When the negotiations broke down and he couldn't purchase the farm, the buggy lost its usefulness. He drove it only a few times in parades. When his barn burned, he decided to sell the buggy to help pay for a new barn.

The three of us plain people, Warren, Susie, and myself, walked into a dusty building where lots of farm equipment was stored. Over against one wall was the buggy. The wheels had been ruined by bugs, and there were holes in the canvas covering. All of the curtains were gone.

Was it salvageable? Warren wasn't sure. And the farmer wasn't sure he wanted to sell it. So I said I would call him back in a few days.

A lot of thoughts ran through my mind during the interim, but I had really decided to buy it. On the appointed day, I called him. He decided to sell the buggy for $200, which was quite a bargain.

So I have the cart, but it's before the horse, so to speak. Now if I can just convince myself to trade my iron horse for one that breathes . . .

Among the Amish

LINDA EGENES

Like the wrinkles of a colorful Amish quilt, the peaks of the Blue Ridge gradually soften into gentle hills by the time you reach Yadkin County, North Carolina. It's along the neatly paved back roads, rising and dipping with the land, that the quiet beauty of spring-green hay fields, rimmed by distant mountains, takes over.

Buck Shoals Road is one of the few here not named for a church, but it compensates by winding past three houses of worship in less than three miles. Right before the road bottoms out in a wooded ravine, I come to a sign that says "ESH'S WOODWORKS." The black buggies tell me I'm in the right spot.

John Esh, the bishop for the Union Grove Amish community, is a serious man who speaks gently. He invites me inside to sit at the kitchen table. Two older daughters are preparing a midmorning snack for their brothers, who work in the family business, building storage barns. Four-year-old Rachel amuses herself by shooting toy arrows around the family room.

John, his wife, and twelve children moved here in 1985 from Franklin County, Pennsylvania. There are twenty families in the community right now, he says, and while half make their living in farming, the other families make storage barns, lawn furniture, or jam.

I ask him if he'd mind talking about his faith and how it enters into everyday life.

"That's what I enjoy talking about most," he says, smiling just a bit.

"We would feel that our faith causes us to be honest in every way, and modest," he says. "It should strengthen us in our efforts. Our longings and desires should be in that direction."

The Amish consider dress to be part of their faith, following a code of rules called the *Ordnung*. John is wearing a handmade denim jacket and pants with suspenders, while his daughters wear long-sleeved dresses that come well below the knee, their hair neatly tucked under white prayer caps. Unlike Old Order Amish communities, the Union Grove Amish use electricity and telephones, and hold their services in a church building instead of their homes. Otherwise their practices are similar, they drive horses and buggies instead of cars, shunning television and all things considered worldly. I ask John if electricity hasn't changed their community.

"As far as I can see, electricity hasn't changed anything. We do stress the simple life the same as other Amish. We have guidelines that keep us from getting too big in business. It is our way of life that strengthens community spirit—a commitment to Christian life, to the plain way."

He says a Catholic family who recently joined the Amish lives up the road, and gives me directions. When I arrive there, Margaret Coletti steps outside the old white farmhouse to greet me. She has dark hair that comes to a slight widow's peak in front, blue eyes, and a vivacious voice full of laughter. She is just two months short of twenty-one. We sit at the kitchen table to chat.

"My parents were active in the Catholic church," she says. "They felt living a Christian life was important, but hard to do in the environment we were in." When I ask her what it was like to adjust to the Amish way of life, she laughs. "I have found peace and contentment in my way of life here. I like the closeness of the Amish way. I feel we have a support system, which the world today sadly lacks.

"Just for example, I'm getting married in September, to an Amish boy from Canada. I needed to make my quilt, but our family's not that great at quilting yet. So the women and girls of the church have come for three different frolics, and it's almost done."

She shows me her quilt, stretched on a frame in the next room, covered with painstakingly tiny stitches. "You have to get seven or eight stitches on the needle at once," she says.

A white outbuilding holds their family bakery, where Margaret helps make pies and breads that they sell wholesale. Chickens peck in the large garden plot that has recently been turned for spring planting; horses graze in a corner of the yard. Her younger brother builds doghouses in a section of the barn that is his workshop. About fifteen completed wooden doghouses sit outside on the lawn, waiting to be picked up.

Margaret thinks it would be fine to drop by a sewing bee, where her mother and other women are spending the day. On my way, I stop at the Yoder Country Market. A horse and open buggy stands outside, and a young Amish woman comes out.

You can tell the people who shop here like to cook from scratch, the old-fashioned way. Seven kinds of flour, eight kinds of beans, eleven different noodles, dried fruits, nuts, and other dry goods line the shelves and low wooden counters. The store sells locally made baked goods, jams, jellies, and pickles—and colorful canned goods from other Amish communities, as well. Devil's claw, chamomile, comfrey, cayenne, licorice root, echinacea, yellow dock root, kelp, chaparral, burdock root, yucca, senna, feverfew, juniper berries, and other herbs fill a corner. *Amish Folk Remedies for Plain and Fancy Ailments,* cookbooks, and hymn books cover the shelf to the right of the cash register, below a selection of broad-brim Amish hats.

David Miller, a man with thoughtful, soft brown eyes, works in the store. "Way more non-Amish come here than Amish," he says when I ask about the customers, "from as far away as Greensboro."

I ask David my electricity question.

"We feel like we put more emphasis on the new birth, on walking with the Lord, rather than on materialism, you might say. It's more practical to use electricity to run the machines of our businesses than converting them to diesel."

Eager to take advantage of the store's low prices, I purchase pecans, dried pineapple, and sweet rolls from the Peachey bakery. David says the rolls are a gift, and won't let me pay for them even when I try.

Leaving the store, I head for the church. There is no sign on the road, only a black mailbox with the number 195 painted on it. I enter the basement, where twenty-five women and teenage girls sit in groups around large quilting frames, assembling comforters. They talk quietly among themselves.

Katie Yoder (the wife of Sam Yoder, who owns the store) shows me around. "A small factory was selling out years ago, and we bought hundreds of bolts of fabric," she says. For the past seven or eight years, the women have met on the second Tuesday of the month to sew. The comforters are sent to Romania and Russia, and any other countries where there is a need.

They average ten comforters in a session. "Sometimes in the evening whole families come, men and boys, too," says Katie. "Then it goes faster."

"We sew strips together first to make blocks of fabric, then we stretch them out on these frames in layers, with batting in the middle," Katie explains, pointing to a large quilt on a frame.

Savannah Miller, a smiling and spry elderly woman, shows me how she draws yellow yarn tassels through the layers to hold the quilts together. "We used to knot them," she says. "But we discovered that if you just loop the yarn through twice, down and up, there is nothing that can pull it apart."

I meet Leah Peachey, who uses a sewing machine to sew a strip around the edges to finish the comforters. She has beautiful light blue eyes, and she smiles softly when she speaks. Her lovely twenty-four-year-old daughter, Orpha, blond hair tucked neatly under her cap, is sewing beside her. When Leah hears that I'd like to visit a farm, she invites me to come to her farm at milking time.

When I comment on how kind they are to do this every month, Katie says, "We've been blessed with so much material, and we do so enjoy getting together."

Just past Windsor's Crossroads live Paul Peachey, his wife, Bertha, and their seven children. When I drive up around four-thirty in the afternoon, Paul and Bertha are sitting outside the storage sheds that hold their jam business, preparing potatoes for planting. Bertha has a bright face and hearty smile, and she shows me how to take a whole potato and cut it into three pieces, making sure each piece has at least three sprouts.

"Each plant will produce a dozen or maybe even twenty potatoes," she says. She tells me they raise almost all their own vegetables on their one-half-acre garden plot, eating fresh in the summer and canning the rest for winter. This spring they will plant peas, potatoes, corn, tomatoes, and all kinds of beans—lima, string, navy, and pinto.

I ask Paul to show me around the jam house. The jam-making kitchen smells sugary, and Paul's daughter Rebecca is wiping down the counters while her sister washes pots. Paul shows me the small stainless-steel kettles they cook the jam in. "We cook it in small batches to maintain consistency," he says.

Bertha joins us in the office. Her youngest son, Paul David, leans against her, and she puts her arms around him. "It isn't what we want to do all our lives," says Paul. "We hope to eventually be on a farm. That would be our desire."

"But until then, it's something we can do as a family," says Bertha.

As we walk outside, Bertha whispers something to Paul. "Would you like to have some jam?" asks Paul. He lets me select one of nine flavors, all labeled "Dutch Kettle," neatly lining the desk. When I choose blackberry, he says that it's his favorite kind, too. Later that night, when my husband and I try the jam, we wish we had bought a crate. It's the only time I've tasted jam as good as my mother's: tangy, sweet, and full of sun-kissed whole berries.

It's getting near milking time, so I head down a long winding road that leads to the large hilltop farm owned by Thomas Peachey, Paul's brother.

A woman with a black woolen scarf over her head and shoulders is walking around the yard with a pitchfork. She waves, and I realize it's Leah Peachey. She says, "I didn't mean to scare you, but I was just turning over some of the dirt in my garden. I came home from sewing and my eleven-year-old son was out there digging up the garden." She had told him he could have his own plot this year.

We walk over to the barn. "I'm always missing things over at the house. I can't see the barn from there like I could at our old farm." She and her husband were born and raised on dairy farms. Now she comes out when she can to help the younger children with their chores, just to be part of it.

Inside the milking room, Rachel and Nathan help their father, Thomas, milk eight holsteins. It takes from five o'clock to seven, morning and evening, to milk the Peacheys' eighty cows, even with machines. The family also raises corn, soybeans, and hay to feed the cows and as cash crops.

The milking machines are clanging away, but Leah speaks as quietly as if we were in her living room. Like all Amish, she speaks German dialect at home, and she says she is not used to speaking in English. But her words, so simple and sincere, express her thoughts eloquently.

"I know no other life," says Leah. "I wouldn't know how to live without a farm. I think you feel closer to God when you work with nature. I'm sure it's the same when you learn any skill or job. Each person has their own way to enrich their life and walk close to God. But on a farm, you can see that God is in all things that are alive and growing."

We move out of the way to let the cows amble out and the next eight come in. "They don't like to be pushed," says Leah. "Have you ever heard it said that contented cows give better milk?"

Leah asks me if I would like to meet her mother, Amelia, who lives in a mobile home near the barn. She is seventy-four years old and is out in the garden working with the soil. "She won't let us do it for her. It's just as much fun for her to garden as it is for the children to play volleyball." Leah shows me how her mother digs a trench, fills it with calf manure, and then covers the trench by digging a new one beside it. "This makes the best soil," says Leah. "My mother gets so many vegetables from her little plot, she gives them away to us."

Amelia asks me inside. I go up the steps to the house first, and offer to help her up. "I'm very independent," says Amelia cheerfully. "I have arthritis in both knees, but I just have to get up my own way."

Inside her cozy trailer, she asks me to sign her guest book. It's nearly full, and the first entry was only 1987. I can see why Amelia has many guests. Her kindly, smiling face makes me feel at home. As we chat, the day fades into darkness, and a warm feeling of family comes to me.

After a buggy ride and tour of Orpha's tidy bakery, I reluctantly bid them good-bye. "We'll think of you as a friend," says Leah. I can't think of anything I'd like more.

The Shakers of Sabbathday Lake

Mary Ann Lieser

It is a hot July morning as we sit in the two-hundred-year-old meetinghouse at Sabbathday Lake, Maine. We have come this Sunday morning to share in worship with the Shakers who live here and with their visitors. The meetinghouse is a large, simple room filled with light from many windows. When the Shakers sing, the room is filled with such rich and full sound that I find myself counting the heads of those who are singing. These few people couldn't possibly fill this room with such a song of praise. It sounds like a choir of angels.

But these few can indeed fill the room with a joyful noise, and they do. And they would say that they have a choir of angels helping them. Eldress Frances Carr tells us later that she feels the very real presence of many other Shakers who have lived and died at Sabbathday Lake when the brothers and sisters come together for worship in the meetinghouse.

Before meeting, the room is quiet, save for the echoes of footsteps on the wooden floor as Shakers and visitors enter and find seats on one of the benches, men on one side and women on the other. Then the elder and eldress leave their dwelling house across the road. They lift the latch and enter the gate, he on the men's side and she on the women's. They come up the steps and find their places and worship begins.

There are readings from both the Old and New Testaments ar

testimony is given. Midway through, meeting is opened for sharing from anyone, and Elder Arnold Hadd encourages each of us to share without hesitation if we feel called to do so, reminding us that their foundress, Mother Ann Lee, said that "a strange gift never came from God." All of the Shakers and many of the dozen or so visitors here this morning do share their concerns or their reflections on the Scripture readings. And, indeed, none of these gifts are "strange," but blend together to form a more complete whole. It is an hour in which we feel we are living in sacred time.

Interspersed throughout is song. The words and music of the simple songs the Shakers sing were written by other Shakers. There are over ten thousand Shaker songs in existence. Many others have been lost, never captured in the written record. The Shakers have several songbooks that they use, and a copy of one of them sits beside each place on the benches in the meetinghouse. But it soon becomes obvious that the eight remaining Shakers who live here carry most of their music in their hearts and can sing it by heart with little prompting. Often during meeting, one of them will begin a song in response to the last person's sharing and almost immediately the others pick up the tune and fill the room with their angelic voices.

The room echoes with footsteps again when meeting is over. Outside in the bright sunshine, Shakers and visitors greet each other warmly. Some visitors say good-bye; others, friends of the community, agree to stay for dinner. We visit over coffee and doughnuts in the dining room while last-minute preparations are completed. The Shaker family's two dogs, Landon and Jason, very much a part of the family themselves, lie at our feet.

My children are restless indoors on such a summery day, so Brother Wayne offers to give our family a tour of the barns and introduce us to the flock of sheep which are his main responsibility, along with keeping the family's woodboxes full during the cold months.

Back indoors, after a silent grace, we eat together. Dinner is a delicious treat of chicken, rice, green beans, and onions, all flavored unforgettably with the herbs for which the Shakers are known. There are fresh strawberries for dessert, and afterward the whole family pitches in to clean up and handle the dishes.

Mother Ann Lee and eight fellow Shakers left England and arrived in New York in 1774 to find a new homeland where they would be free to practice their spiritual beliefs without persecution. They found fertile ground, and during the next fifty years their numbers increased to over five thousand Shakers living in more than a dozen communities. The Shaker villages, scattered throughout New England and the Midwest, were fairly self-sufficient, engaging in both agricultural and craft production, and trading among themselves for items in which particular villages specialized. Converts who embraced the Shaker faith and life gave up their earthly possessions and their earthly family to become part of the Shaker family. All Shakers are brothers and sisters in Christ and live with a commitment to celibacy and communalism.

The Shakers declined in numbers following the Civil War, and villages began dissolving or combining with one another as their members became too few or too aged to carry on. Today, the village at Sabbathday Lake is the only remaining Shaker village in which brothers and sisters dwell. Shakerdom accepted no new members for some years, when the ministry was located in Canterbury, New Hampshire. The eldresses there had decided to close themselves to new applicants. Although those at Sabbathday Lake were eager to embrace newer and younger believers, they abided by the decision rendered at Canterbury in order to preserve harmony among the faithful. With the passing of the last Shakers at Canterbury, the leaders at Sabbathday Lake opened their family to sincere seekers willing to embrace their faith and way of life. Half of their present number of eight have joined within the last fifteen years, and three of these are in their thirties.

Although the community is open to new members, those interested in joining must first spend a good deal of time getting acquainted, a time of trial to determine whether the fit is right for both the family and the prospective member. The relationship often begins by correspondence. A series of weekend visits follows. The seeker then undertakes a novitiate of one year, living as a member of the community during that time, before becoming a Shaker brother or sister.

Later in the week, it is another hot and humid afternoon as we sit in the music room in the main dwellinghouse, built in 1795. The sound of cars on the highway not far from where we sit is a contemporary contrast to the furnishings in this room, many of them antique or original. The Shaker family at Sabbathday Lake has adopted many modern conveniences, from electricity to computers, at the same time that they have retained much from their Shaker tradition. The sisters still wear the traditional plain cape dress to worship on Sunday mornings, and some wear it at other times, as well.

This day, Elder Arnold Hadd and Eldress Frances Carr have graciously taken some time to talk with us. This is a hectic week for them. As well as being in the middle of the busy summer season when many visitors come to tour their Shaker family home, today they are preparing for an influx of guests arriving for a conference that begins in two days, commemorating this community's bicentennial.

During our visit a young girl named Joy, who had waited on us earlier in the Shaker store, pops in to report to Sister Frances that she has managed to bake 485 cookies today in preparation for the conference. Overseeing the work of the kitchen is one of the many jobs that Sister Frances capably fills. She tells us that they used to rotate jobs when she was a young woman living in this community.

When she first began learning the kitchen routine at Sabbathday Lake, each sister who worked in the kitchen spent two weeks there, alternating with two weeks of nonkitchen duties. With eight members now, tasks have become more permanent.

Two sisters do the bulk of the cooking and kitchen work for the family. One brother handles most of the community's correspondence and typesets their publication, the *Shaker Quarterly*. One sister puts in many hours in the Shaker library, located on the grounds. Another sister handles most of the community's extensive herb gardens, with the help of a full-time gardener hired for the busy summer months. The community produces a wide array of herbs that are dried and packaged in tins to be sold either in the store, which is open during the summer, or year-round through their mail-order catalog. The proceeds from the sale of herbs provide one of the community's main sources of income.

"Hands to work, hearts to God," Mother Ann told the Shakers two hundred years ago, and the family at Sabbathday Lake still lives by that precept on a daily basis. Work here is a duty and a privilege. The oldest and most frail family members are valued and loved and still contribute as they are able. The oldest sister is eighty-seven and still knits items to be sold in the Shaker store.

Though they are somewhat separated during their working hours when each Shaker attends to his or her familiar routine of tasks, the family is reunited several times during the day for periods of shared worship, prayer, and reflection. After breakfast, they gather for morning prayers, including a responsive reading of two Psalms and Old and New Testament readings. They gather again at eleven-thirty for a quiet time in the prayer room before the midday meal. And on Wednesday afternoons at five-thirty they meet in the meetinghouse for midweek worship.

One soon realizes that though there may be only eight Shakers living here, this family forms the very strong core of a much larger spiritual community. Brother Arnold explains that the Bible passages read during morning prayers are chosen in advance and sent to each one of a group of people known to the Shaker family as Friends of the Holy Spirit. These scattered friends have visited Sabbathday Lake at various times. They feel spiritual ties and strong bonds of kinship with the Shakers but, because of family responsibilities or other commitments, cannot be Shakers themselves. So the Shakers have reached out to form a larger circle that embraces these far-flung friends.

Other friends of the Shakers visit often to share worship and a meal, and the family at Sabbathday Lake cherishes these friends, as well. Although the monastic life may not be right for them, they are a valuable part of the Shaker extended family.

As the community of believers at Sabbathday Lake embarks upon their third century in this place, there is a sense of expectancy. Though their number may be small, they have held steady for several decades, and the average age of individuals is actually younger now than it has been in half a century. Hope for the future, and for light and life to continue to fill these houses that have been filled with believers for two hundred years, is strong. That hope stands alongside a deep commitment to accept God's will, whatever the future brings. It is adjacent to the calm routine of daily work that gives shape to the lives of the people who abide here.

And infusing everything is a strong sense of love and graciousness. Sister Frances embraces us as we bid farewell, and will not let us leave without a gift. But we know well that the best gift we've received is the chance to be welcomed by this Shaker family and to share in their love and their gratitude as they sing their angelic songs of praise.

The Crowded Island

Franklin Saige

It wasn't hard to spot me during my first trip to New York City last autumn. As a representative of *Homo sapiens hayseed*, I spent most of my two days there either looking up at the buildings from down in the street, or looking down at the teeming streets from up in the buildings.

Just about anything I could tell you about my experience would merely highlight my contemptible parochialism. In such a short time, I honestly didn't learn very much about the real joys and sorrows of city life.

Even so, I couldn't help but notice that there were several million people there, packed onto a piece of land no bigger than the rural county where I grew up.

My first reaction to this was wonder at the technology that allows for so many people to inhabit such a small area. This was a looking-up-at-the-buildings thought.

My next insight, however, was that it is not a good idea for people to live on top of one another. A looking-down-at-the-street thought, to be sure. I had my share of weird and abrasive New York encounters, along with all the nice experiences. Nothing special, but also nothing like my home in Hayseed, USA.

I note these (only slightly informed) reactions because they direct one pole of my concern with the environmental threat from overpopulation.

I'm interested in the "economies of scale" at work in the big city, because environmentalists tell us that if we can't start right away to lower the number of people, cities offer the only hope for saving the land. Massing people together in cities supposedly confers structural benefits that can lessen waste and reduce the conversion of world stuff (resources) into people stuff (consumables). This happens, for instance, when folks walk or take public transit to shop, because the shopping is nearby.

In my brief visit, however, I observed that for New Yorkers, this same structure of convenience results in a concentration and enlargement of consumption, not its diminution. *Madison Avenue* is not just a phrase used to describe the manipulation of needs and wants; it's a street in New York City, and at street level it dispenses an empty, acquisitive lifestyle of class and fashion.

This permanently frantic display of goods seems to be an end product of putting people together in a hoped-for efficiency of bigness. It reminds me (hayseed that I am) of the "efficiencies" of modern, monoculture farming.

Unlike the Amish agriculture prevalent in my neighborhood, high-tech, no-till farming substitutes expensive, soil-compacting machines and expensive, toxic chemicals for the community of people, livestock, horses, and diversified crops. This efficiency of ends comes with a heavy price for the land, however. Researchers at Oberlin College have found, for instance, that "Amish dirt"—with its rotated crops and repeated applications of manure and straw from the barn—absorbs and holds more than six times as much water as the average no-till field.

To me, it does not make sense to grow more food on less land, if in the process the land is destroyed and the food is poisoned, any more than it makes sense to pile people together in the name of conservation, when this results in their becoming hyperconsumers.

I would not go so far as to say that the management of dense populations must always result in the "inefficient efficiencies" that erode American culture in the same way the technological war on agriculture is dooming American soil.

It is just a question I am asking myself, one pole, as I said, of my thinking through of an issue that is becoming an ever greater part of the environmental movement's activism. I wouldn't be asking myself about the pitfalls of managing population density if I didn't have an even greater fear of the other pole: the belief that fewer people, not better approaches to managing their impact, is the solution to the world's problems.

As with my recent trip to New York, I haven't spent a whole lot of time studying the rhetoric of population control. I have stumbled onto the basic formula that expresses the supposed efficiency of the approach: $I = PAT$. Invented by Paul Erlich, $I = PAT$ means the Impact (I) of people on the ecological well-being of the world is the Population (P) multiplied by the Amount (A) of goods consumed per person multiplied by the pollution generated by the Technology (T) per good consumed.

$I = PAT$ is the formula of choice for population activists and environmentalists. From it they have deduced a solution. Control human reproduction.

Just a stone's throw away from where I walked the canyons of New York City, the United Nations and the World Health Organization have put $I = PAT$ at the center of international family-planning programs. A very few people have questioned $I = PAT$ from a number of perspectives (see *Taking Population out of the Equation* [North Amherst, Mass.: Institute on Women and Technology, 1993] by H. Patricia Hynes), usually along the lines of asking why population should have the same multiplying power as consumption and technology. After all, aren't there people who partake very little

of the fruits of industrial civilization? How is reducing their numbers a good thing?

To which I would add, Where is the algebraic symbol for the
healthy soil Amish agriculture is building in formerly farmed-
out or marginal land? This is a good thing, this Dirt (D), and it
ought to be in the formula, too: $I=(P-D)AT$, where D means that
every ton of topsoil added reduces the population impact by one
person.

There, we've saved thousands of people from being depopulated!

I read through an environmental magazine on the train ride home
from New York. The lead article was entitled "The Environmental
Consequences of Having a Baby in the United States." As my train
chugged through the sparsely settled contours of the Appalachians,
I read that, "Some religious sects promote unrestrained procreation," and that, "the arrival of a new baby is usually considered a
wonderful event, as indeed it is; but from the perspectives of the
world's natural ecosystems, another human being means additional
strains on already severely strained resources."

The article presented a comprehensive set of statistics to show
that Americans consume huge amounts of natural resources; nowhere did this seem to suggest that lifestyle, rather than population
control, should be the first line of inquiry.

"Many Americans are looking for ways they can help protect the
environment. The success of such aspirations will be influenced by
American economic processes, government regulations, cultural attitudes, educational orientations, and technological advances and
limitations, *which are outside the control of most individuals*." [empha-
sis added]

I think my plain-living family of five's resource use is approximately one-fifth of the average American family of four. If I am given a choice, I would much prefer changing those things that are supposedly out of my control to eliminating any of my children. It seems like a smaller sacrifice.

And so my mood grew ever gloomier, as the scientifically couched paper added its own rather chilling twist. Parents were charged to regard the essay as an environmental impact statement for childbirth, and respond accordingly.

If we are going to accept impact statements as the basis for family planning, why involve parents? The government or the World Health Organization, for that matter, could just as well implement such controls over us. Probably more efficiently, in fact.

Even as I sent this scientifically dressed-up pogrom through the shredder, I had to admit that I, too, am concerned about the growth in world population, and how this is damaging ecosystems. However, before the population-reduction people start throwing my people in jail, I would like to reply with two points on behalf of those "religious sects [who] promote unrestrained procreation":

1. The state I live in has been losing population for at least the last three decades. And still, the urban and suburban areas have expanded to many times their previous sizes, grinding up good farmland, wetlands, and natural habitat to make strip malls, golf courses, strip malls, freeways, strip malls, strip malls, strip malls. Where I live, what has grown exponentially in the last thirty years is greed, not population.

2. The typical Amish family of eight, living today, isn't spending much if any time driving to the nearest strip mall. They aren't burning holes in the ozone layer or buying beef from the rain forest. On the contrary, it's likely they are reclaiming damaged land and building topsoil like there's no tomorrow. Make no mistake, their

numbers *are* growing exponentially. Their fertile hoard swarms right up to the border of encroaching suburbia. When this sorry world is filled up with these radical Christians, will the planet be worse off? Given their religiously based fondness for community and their ability to assimilate the heart's love with the hand's work, what will the Amish megalopolis be like?

The Place Where We Live

MARY ANN LIESER

I live in a town that is known throughout our local area for its preservation of old buildings and its sense of history. That sense of history is one of the things that brought my family here three years ago.

We live in the Western Reserve area of Ohio, which was once the western territory deeded to settlers from Connecticut. Many of the small towns here were patterned after those of New England, with a large open commons, or village green, in the town's center.

But few of our neighboring towns still have an intact village center. One township to the east, the green is now broken into four quadrants by the intersection of two highways—one of them five lanes wide—and is ringed by fast-food restaurants. Two townships to the south, the village green is now a never-used patch of grass surrounded by a traffic circle that is almost always full of cars. But our town has always been preservation-minded and has seen to it that large sections of the green are still pleasing to the eye and useful to the town. In one section is a white gazebo where band concerts are held every Sunday evening throughout the summer. Another section has trees and benches. Because it is safe and easy to walk to, it is often occupied by children playing or bicyclists and pedestrians resting on the benches.

My family lives two blocks from the village green in a small hundred-year-old home. Many of our neighbors' houses in this section of town bear plaques from the local heritage association. It is an area steeped in history and a sense of place.

Four blocks to our north is the township's original cemetery, dedicated in 1808. I often stop there when I'm out with my children for a walk. They run in the grass and try to climb the trees while I read the inscriptions on the stones. At least one Revolutionary War veteran is buried here. The last burial took place in 1900.

Many of the things that drew us to this historic town, however, no longer compel us to stay. We have begun looking for a house and land in a more rural area where we believe it will be easier to pass our values on to our children. We have changed in many ways during the time we've lived here, and we've watched this town change, too.

I like to walk in my neighborhood, and I enjoy looking at the gardens and the houses. I often walk downtown, as well, just on the other side of the green, to run errands. I can handle many errands within a short walk of home. Bank, library, post office, and drugstore are all within two blocks; the grocery and hardware store are an additional half mile.

The walk is infinitely more enjoyable than driving and parking a car would be. But often, I feel as if I'm living in a museum or a very large movie set. Stray two blocks outside the historic section of town, and a different reality prevails. This township has been rapidly developed by the building industry during the past twenty years, and continues to be today. The charm of the old village attracts many people who want to live here. Virtually any home built in the township will find a buyer quickly. There is almost no open land left anywhere in the area.

In place of the diversity that could be found here several decades ago, with open fields and woodlands separating the old farmhouses and fledgling housing developments, virtually every available lot is now a building site. The wall-to-wall housing developments, unrelieved by meadow, forest growth, or any open space save for a few city-maintained ball diamonds, leaves an impression of monotonous uniformity.

And all of these housing tracts spill their traffic onto the same few thoroughfares, causing congestion in the heart of town during business hours and spillover traffic on my street at the busiest times.

Last summer my family and I visited a "historic village" that lies less than ten miles from here. Houses and buildings have been restored and moved to an old farm. Filled with antique tools and furnishings, they comprise a village typical of the mid–nineteenth century. Costumed tour guides are stationed in each building, be it school, church, law office, spinning and weaving shop, or dwelling, to offer a brief overview of life 150 years ago.

This place follows the village-green model, with a large expanse of grass in the center. A path wide enough for vehicles surrounds the green, and the shops and dwellings open onto that path. The village also includes the buildings and animals typical of a nineteenth-century farm, and these can be found beyond the inner ring that circles the green.

The attitude of both visitors and employees is one of nostalgia, and perhaps condescension, as they view the quaint beginnings of the places they will go home to. But on the day I visited, I couldn't help but notice how well this village-green model worked. Houses were interspersed with shops, a school, and all else necessary to fill the needs of the residents. The surrounding farms would also use a village's shops and services. The open space in the center of town provided common ground—a place where people could gather. By preserving open land in the heart of the village, the green provided a natural limit to growth. When the outlying areas could no longer be comfortably serviced by a village, a new one would be started a few miles away. The result was compact population growth, rather than the suburban sprawl that has overtaken the present-day Western Reserve. But the village we visited, with all its advantages, is only a museum. Nobody will ever live there.

The "common ground" of our ancestors has been destroyed by the automobile. The car is the primary reason virtually every town's green in this area is an inaccessible and unused relic. And even this town I live in, where people have fought so hard to preserve vestiges of a way of life that is all but gone, even this town is being destroyed.

I don't have the answers to the questions I have about what can be done to make this place as much of a town as it was a hundred years ago.

But everywhere I look I see a steady stream of cars, funneled from dozens of housing developments onto one of the few through streets, and it seems obvious to me that what we're doing here isn't working. I have come to believe that it is very difficult, perhaps impossible, to have real community in a place where most of the people do their traveling by car.

During the past three years I've watched this place disappear, a little more all the time, and I can't help but wonder how long it will be before the heart and soul of our town, as represented by its vibrant village green, is no longer needed.

Better than Fixing Things

ELMO STOLL

The story is told of a man from the big city who moved to the country. It happened that the house and lot he bought were right in the middle of a community of plain people. The big-city man was a bit apprehensive about these bearded men who had no power lines connected to their buildings and who drove to town behind the clip-clop of horse hooves. But he assured himself that they looked gentle enough, and he had always heard that although they were different, they were quite harmless.

He was reassured on moving day when one of his plain neighbors showed up to help him unload his many belongings. The neighbor's strong back and willing muscles came in handy, as without comment he helped carry in the usual North American assortment of electrical appliances and labor-saving, comfort-producing gadgets. That evening before leaving for his home, the plain man motioned toward all the appliances he had helped unload, and said to the big-city man, "Now if any of these things break down, don't hesitate to let me know, and I'll come over."

The man from the big city was completely taken by surprise, but quite pleased. "Oh, that's nice," he exclaimed. "Do you fix things?"

"No," said the plain man. "I have no idea how to fix these things. But I will be happy to show you how to live without them."

Perhaps that story explains our perspective quite well. We see a lot of people whose lives revolve around possessions that are intended to make life easy for them. A growing number of these people are concerned about the environmental impact of their lifestyles. A few are concerned about the spiritual impact. But no real solutions can be found as long as people are not willing to accept self-discipline and measures of sacrifice and restraint. The search seems to focus on how to live a lavish lifestyle without suffering bad effects. We feel the solution is to change the lifestyle.

Many plain communities today are approached by a steady stream of disenchanted people from mainstream society looking for alternatives. These "seekers," as they have come to be known, arrive in an assorted package. Some know what they are looking for, and some know what they are running from. A few have a clearly defined sense of both; others, neither. They range in culture, education, intellect, sincerity, commitment, and wealth from one end of the spectrum to the other.

For most plain people, who traditionally have found some refuge in simply avoiding change, this deluge of seekers knocking on their doors is in itself a change. And some find it a threatening sort of change they hardly know how to deal with. Others seek, with varying degrees of success, to rise to the challenge.

One of the most prevalent myths about the plain people is that you have to be born into a plain community, or you are forever locked out. This is simply not true. Although some plain groups are less open to converts than others are, I know of none that will turn away someone who is willing to do whatever is required of him.

Due to a variety of complex factors, some communities attract more seekers than others do. Our community here in the hills of rural Tennessee has an unusually high proportion of people who did not grow up in a horse-and-buggy, nonelectrical lifestyle. In fact, many plain people in other communities have come to believe that helping seekers is our purpose for existing, and it is not uncommon for them to refer their seekers to us. We do not object to having people sent our way—only to the assumptions that plain people can always give help and that the rest need it. These seekers often end up helping us as much as we help them. It would be arrogant for us to suppose that we have all the answers and that we can help others. And in the final analysis, all of Christ's disciples, regardless of their backgrounds, are bidden to be seekers: "Seek ye first the kingdom of God and His righteousness . . ." (Matthew 6:33).

The community here in Cookeville was started four years ago by a small core of Amish and Mennonite families. Disturbed by the growing financial burden most plain communities are facing in their efforts to maintain family-size farms for everyone in the face of escalating land costs, we pooled our resources and purchased a two-hundred-acre tract of land that is shared communally. We would rather work harder to make do with less land than see any of our brethren assume a debt burden. Presently sixteen families are living on this property and three more on nearby rented properties. Because tillable land is at a premium, we concentrate on doing things and growing crops that are labor intensive and have a high return per acre. Perhaps half of us or more are in vegetable and truck-crop production, growing especially tomatoes, cantaloupes, melons, strawberries, and peppers. Raising cane for the cooking of sorghum molasses is also a major crop; it lends itself well to our ideals: easy to grow without sprays and chemicals, low investment per acre, and can be harvested by the community working together with just man and horse power.

We try to grow as much of our own food as we can. Not having refrigeration, we need to can or dry food that is put by for off-season use. The crops we grow for resale are marketed both wholesale and retail. We operate a retail market at the edge of the community to which customers can come at regular business hours six days a week and purchase items grown or produced within the community. Besides produce and sorghum, we also have baked items, honey, and furniture. Near the retail market is a harness shop where one of our number makes harnesses and repairs both harnesses and saddles. The community also has a blacksmith, a baker, a cabinetmaker, a shoemaker, a sign painter, and a farrier.

Our community has chosen to limit the use of internal combustion engines. The only means of travel we own are horse drawn or human pedaled. We have no rule against hiring someone to haul something for us by motor vehicle or to take us somewhere if the distance is too great to go by horse or bicycle, but we like to keep these occasions from becoming frequent or routine. We ride Greyhound buses quite a bit. We do not take the position that modern technology is evil in itself, but we would like to be in control of it, rather than having it control us.

It seems as though the entire world is on board a train that is speeding rapidly downhill, picking up momentum all the time, and although many are dismayed at the direction they are traveling, they seemingly can find no way to safely jump off.

Is it possible that people can be controlled by something, yet still in their minds cling to the illusion that they are firmly in the driver's seat? Listen to the following confession that could come from the lips of a typical North American.

"The things I own are just tools. My car is just a way to get to where I want to go. These modern things don't control me; I control them. For example, I use my car for good things. With it I can go visit my mother in the old folks' home twice a week."

"Old folks' home? Why is your mother in there?"

"She gets good care there. We couldn't take care of her at home. My wife and I both work. It's difficult enough to get someone to stay with the children when we are both gone at the same time."

How sad. For generations, simple common folks with just hand tools were able to find time to care for their children and their old folks at home. Now, with all these inventions and labor-saving devices, we don't have time to care for our ailing parents. What has brought about this change? Was it really an improvement over the day of the extended family when generations overlapped, and there was a place and need for all?

We live in a world given over to professionalism. This pattern is established the day a typical North American is born. He comes into the world in a sterile delivery room under bright lights, attended by a professional. When he dies, a professional is hired to wash him up, embalm him, clothe him, provide a casket, and bury him. There is little concept that a person could or should maintain control over his life and do things for himself. People are taught that they are not able or adequate to do things themselves, and this teaching very quickly becomes self-fulfilling. Although we still have a long way to go, we here at the community struggle to regain this control once again, from the time our babies are born to when our bodies need burial.

Education is another realm where we put our foot down. About half of the community's children attend a one-room eight-grade classroom, while the remainder are schooled at home by their parents. If parents are able and willing to teach their children at home, that is fine; if not, the community school is provided for the rest.

School starts early—at seven-thirty A.M.—and runs to a late noon—twelve-thirty. Then the children go home to eat lunch with their families, and devote all afternoon to learning how to work at something useful with their hands. Head knowledge has its place, but most people in North America would be better off with a few more callouses on their hands.

Although we disdain the "rat race," where people dash everywhere and get nowhere, we would not like to conjure up in your mind any romantic notions of lazy afternoons yawning under shade trees. We spend much of our time mopping our brows, laboring in the sun. We make no apology about working hard. If you're looking for a free ride or an easy way, please go somewhere else. Cutting your firewood with a crosscut or doing the laundry in a hand-powered tub involves sweat and tired muscles. But it does help keep the children occupied and for us adults is generally good for the soul.

People who have been observing us and trying to figure out whether we believe in private property or community of goods have come to suspect us of schizophrenia. It's just that we don't fit into any of the usual slots—either the common purse of Hutterites, or the private property of the Amish and Mennonites. Instead we aim for a balance between individual responsibility and total sharing that we feel squarely reflects the Gospel message and the example of the early church.

Unlike a typical Amish group, we do believe in going out to proclaim the Gospel. But in reality our "going out" so far has been limited, as we have needed to spend most of our time with those "coming in." And one way we have sought to spread the good news of the kingdom has been to establish small communities in new neighborhoods. It does not require a lot of discernment to see that some of the problems of standard Amish society result from communities being allowed to get too big. From the beginning we resolved that we would not permit ourselves to make the same mistake. (My father used to shake his head at the huge Amish settlements and say that even honeybees have enough sense to swarm when a hive gets crowded.)

As a result, when the Cookeville community became overpopulated, we started a new community New Decatur, Tennessee, and now more recently a fledgling community in New Brunswick, Canada.

How do people find out about us? By word of mouth mostly and, also, we do publish, as time and resources allow, a community paper called *Update*. It generally contains news of what is happening, an article or two explaining what we believe and how we think, and feedback letters from our readers. Since we usually print names and addresses of those who write to us, our little paper has become one means by which scattered individuals and families across the nation find each other.

One day King David, reminiscing about his boyhood, mentioned to his men how good that water used to taste from the well in Bethlehem. Two of his loyal men conceived a brave but dangerous plan. They sneaked down that night and, at the risk of their lives, drew water from under the very noses of the guarding Philistine soldiers, and brought it back to David. Instead of gulping down the water for his own enjoyment, David poured it on the ground as an offering to God. That little story from the Old Testament sounds ridiculous to most people today. We live in a world that has lost a concept of sacrifice; water poured on the ground before God seems like a waste. Only if we drink it ourselves do people count it as worthwhile. And yet to live in community and brotherhood, this whole way of thinking that centers on self-expression and self-enjoyment must change. We need to find meaning and worth in dying to self and living in submission to others.

The taste of modern society is sweet today in people's mouths, but it is causing severe pains in the stomach. None like the stomachache, but few are willing to give up the sweet taste. Here is an illustration: A man came to us with a young daughter, looking for refuge from a world that had broken his heart and ruined his life. We hurt for him as he related the unhappy details of how his wife had left him for another man. He admired the emphasis he saw among us on a committed family life. It did not take him long to know that this was the kind of community he wanted his daughter to grow up in. But before he made the final decision to come in our direction, he had one question to check out: Would we allow him to remarry?

When we told him, as we understood the Bible, it would not be right for him to marry again as long as his wife lived, he turned sadly away. He wanted the benefits of a society where people lived with integrity and commitment, but if he had to have it at the cost of living that way himself, he was not willing to pay the price.

It is simply an unalterable fact of life that although we are free to make our choices, we cannot choose which set of consequences will follow the choices we make. The Apostle Paul called it reaping what we sow.

We don't claim to have all the answers. We only profess to know Him who has them. We have made our share of mistakes, and no doubt we will make many more. We have had to learn some lessons the hard way. Of ourselves we have nothing to boast. But we cannot be silent when all around us we see people trapped and held in bondage by forces from which they do not know how to escape. If you do not like where you are headed, but think there are no other choices, gather up fresh hope. We may not know how to fix all the broken things in your life, but working together with God's help, we may be able to find ways for you to live without them.

A Farming Community

DAVID KLINE

The past two weeks have been busy with silo filling. The drought (half an inch of rain in July and three-tenths in August) dried off the corn much earlier than was expected, and all of a sudden every farmer's crop, even the late-planted corn, was ready to be cut. Since the seven neighbors who make up our crew also help outward into other filling rings, it took a lot of planning and date changing until everyone had their date set.

We filled ours yesterday forenoon. By eleven o'clock the bundles of corn in the three-acre field were cut and in the silo. After the teams were unhitched, put in the barn, and fed, we washed up and ate dinner.

There is something about hard work, along with the cooler weather, that builds an appetite. But Elsie and the girls were well prepared for the hungry bunch—potatoes, corn, beef, coleslaw, sliced tomatoes, and melons, along with several dandy desserts. Since we were finished early and had an early dinner, we sat around the table and visited for another hour before the neighbors in-spanned their teams and went home.

All of the neighbors that helped us were Amish. However, as recently as three or four decades ago that wasn't the case. Then all neighbors, whether Catholic or Methodist or Quaker or Lutheran or Amish, needed and helped each other.

———

My parents were married in January of 1929 and moved to this neighborhood in February—a neighborhood that was largely French Catholic but also included some Protestant families along with a scattering of Amish families. This diversity of religious beliefs did not hinder the families from working together. They needed each other. Not every art and skill needed for rural living was known by every person in the community. So the people who had a particular art or skill in their possession shared it with their neighbors.

Father died late last winter. He was eighty-seven. For sixty-seven years he was a part of this community. He became ill last fall and after numerous tests was diagnosed with cancer of the colon. During surgery in December the doctor found that the tumor was inoperable and a bypass was performed instead.

Soon after Father regained consciousness he asked me, "Do the neighbors know about my illness? Do they ask how I'm coming along?" I assured him that they all knew and not a day passed that someone didn't stop by to ask how he was getting along and when he was coming home. Then I added, "Do you know why, Dad? It is because you gave yourself so selflessly to the community all these years. Maybe you aren't aware of it, but there is a saying, 'You can't give yourself away.' " We held each other and wept.

Father was one of those rare people who possessed many of the arts and skills needed in thriving rural communities. Besides being a farmer and husbandman, he was a thresherman (a title that also included silo filling, corn husking with the machine, fodder shredding, and clover hulling), a sawyer, an orchardist, his own mechanic, a carpenter (he could design and build anything from kitchen cabinets to mortise-and-tenon frame buildings), for a short time his own blacksmith, plumber, and for a while he even whitewashed our milking stable using the orchard sprayer. His stiff lime-covered coat still hangs from a spike on the shop wall. These talents he freely shared with the neighbors.

After a hospital stay of fifteen days we brought Father home where, from a bed in the living room, he could look out across the familiar fields and neighborhood instead of gazing at shopping center roofs and parking lots.

Since we live on the home farm I was at Father's bedside much of the time through his four months' illness. When he felt up to it we talked. Father kept a diary from 1941 through 1943 and then from 1949 to early 1959. I had never read his diaries, but now I got them out of his desk and read them, sometimes out loud to him. Yes, yes, he remembered. And then he would begin reminiscing about how he started threshing for the neighbors, first for five neighbors who owned the threshing machine in partnership. Eventually the threshing ring included over twenty farms.

From reading the diaries I was astonished at the number of days Father spent helping neighbors. For example, one week in November of 1943 showed him at a different neighbor's farm every day.

Monday: *Husked corn at John Rothacker's.* [A Lutheran family]
Tuesday: *Helped Mrs. Miller.* [Her husband was in a mental hospital.]
Wednesday: *Helped Eli cut logs.* [Amish]
Thursday: *Husked corn for Mrs. Dan Kaufman.* [A widow]
Friday: *Husked corn for Clarence Besancon.* [Catholic]
Saturday: *Husked corn for Levi Kuhns.* [Conservative Mennonite]

Naturally, Father and the neighbors helping to do the work would eat the noon meal with the farm family where the work was done. He would often talk about the excellent cooks they encountered throughout the community. In the fall, once the sweet potatoes were ready,

Pearl Stutz could prepare candied yams no one could match. It seemed every farm wife had one special dish she excelled in.

This all began to change soon after the Second World War, when the mechanization of agriculture began to gain momentum. For a while, the Industrial Revolution may have helped to build community, or at least didn't do a great deal to destroy it. For instance, the threshing machine and mechanical corn husker still needed the help of neighbors to operate efficiently. But as the war economy shifted to a peacetime economy, farmers were pressured to modernize and that meant buying bigger and more "efficient" tractors and machinery.

While the Amish resisted this pressure to change, and still do today, so did many of our other neighbors. One of the Catholic farmers, in the late 1940s, sold his farm at auction rather than change to tractor farming. The Lutheran neighbor never cared for the new neighborless farming and still threshed through the late 1950s, until it simply became too unfashionable in his society to do so. With his leaving, an art was lost; he had been one of the best straw stackers in the neighborhood.

I believe it is safe to say that the machine became the great destroyer of community. What was a gradual change up to about 1950 suddenly became an abrupt, almost brutal process. Unfortunately, the acquisition of labor-saving farm machines often had far-reaching effects, even for the plain communities—greater than anyone anticipated, if anyone even was anticipating the harm that could result from the changeover.

As the neighboring farmers began the change to more modern agriculture, fewer of their sons and daughters returned to the farm or the community when they graduated from college, as many of them did. Many went on to successful careers elsewhere. Also, their interests changed. In the past the holy days were always celebrated in the home or at the church with their neighbors and friends. Now there was a shift away to distant places. Likewise, for recreation the themes changed, too.

When most of the American farmers began using the grain combine sometime during the decade of the 1950s, secondhand threshing machines suddenly became cheap. Machines that cost nearly $2,000 in the 1940s now dropped to $300 or $400. And the large twenty-farmer threshing rings disappeared almost overnight. Most were broken into four- to six-farmer rings—which in some ways may have been to the farmer's advantage because it shortened the threshing season and thus lessened the likelihood of rain-damaged grains and straw.

The majority of Amish have attempted to preserve the working together of communities by restricting the use of certain machines on the farm. When the machine in question replaced the need for the help of neighbors, such as the grain combine instead of threshing or the forage chopper instead of silo filling, the church leaders said no, too much will be lost. Even the telephone in the home is rejected in favor of face-to-face communication. (The most conservative group of Amish in our community do not publish their deaths in the newspaper. They notify the neighbors, friends, and relatives in person.) In other words, when the issue is between self and community, community is chosen.

Not all the Amish have the sharing-community view. A small number, even among the most conservative, have chosen not to be part of neighborhood threshing and silo filling. They can do it themselves and have become nonparticipants in the community.

Interestingly, along with this self-reliance comes a different religious view. If these individuals are ministers, their sermons change. There may be a subtle downplaying of plain living. They see a need to point out the dangers of *Werksgerechtigkeit* (works righteousness).

(This usually occurs at about the point where replacing horse traction with fossil-fuel traction is being considered.) A minister may grab the lapels of his coat and emphasize that the plain coat will not get you to Heaven. Rarely in these sermons is any mention made of loving thy neighbor as thyself. The focus is shifted toward the "inward man."

It is not my intention to pass judgments. I am not merely an observer of what is happening to our and other rural communities; I'm a part of the community and as guilty as anyone of making wrong decisions and failing in fulfilling my commitments to the church, neighborhood, and community.

Our community has a broad spectrum of plain and formerly plain churches—as many as twenty different denominations, from the ultraconservative to the ultraliberal. It is interesting to observe the views of the different Anabaptist divisions on the importance of neighboring or of community as the pendulum swings from conserving our church practices to liberalizing them. For the one, it is crucial to their Christian beliefs to work and share together. Self is given for community. For the other, plain living has been discarded, and the idea of community has been reduced to supporting the local basketball team and the fire department, and maybe carpooling to the mall.

To illustrate these opposite views I would like to give the example of two farmers. The one, who is from a plain church that may be shifting from *gemeinshaft* (brotherhood) toward self, made the remark, "We'll cut all our own oats and bale it for hay so we won't have to help the neighbors thresh."

The other one was from a conservative church and in a neighborhood threshing ring where one of the farmers quit and went on his own. He had tears in his eyes when he told me that his neighbor had dropped out. Not because he couldn't get his crops harvested, but that the blessing of helping his neighbor was taken away.

Last year in our autumn communion services, Dad, who was eighty-seven, and Jonas T., who was ninety, washed each other's feet. As first one and then the other bent over the washtub and tenderly observed John 13:14, they were silently telling one another: Even though we have attended the same church and lived in the same community and helped each other for over sixty-three years—our children and some of our grandchildren attending the same school— we still need each other. And before spring communion came, both were in their graves.

Local Sufficiency

BILL DUESING

Reconnecting

Although our home and farm are in the country, we do some of our most important work in New Haven and Bridgeport—two cities on Long Island Sound, about twenty miles away, in different directions.

On our farm, we're turning the soil and using plants and animals to feed ourselves and to create a diverse, sustainable, and nourishing ecosystem. In the cities, we're working as part of a growing network of people and organizations who are turning bureaucracies as well as soil—using plants, animals, and the energy of children and adults to create local, sustainable food systems.

The entrenched bureaucracies of the cities aren't as easy to work with as the soil on our farm or even as degraded urban soils, but the reality of a sustainable future emerges nonetheless.

History

Just forty years ago, these cities were surrounded by small towns with a rich and varied agriculture. Connecticut still produced half of its own food. Milk was delivered in refillable bottles from nearby dairy farms. Pig farmers picked up food wastes from in-ground bins located in every urban home's backyard. Local breweries and bottlers refilled glass bottles. One of our neighbors delivered eggs to mom-and-pop markets in Bridgeport. Truck farmers with environmentally friendly and human-scale operations delivered vegetables and fruits to neighborhood markets, no doubt taking home some goods from the store's bakery in exchange. The city and the country were integrally connected and mutually dependent.

Since the 1950s, suburbs have grown rapidly, as lower taxes, better-equipped schools, open space, and lack of crime encouraged well-off, mostly white folks and businesses to flee the city. This had a negative impact on the tax base in the city as well as on the agricultural base in the country. Beautiful, well-made factories and fabulous Victorian houses were boarded up or torn down in the cities. Grand old barns, elegant chicken houses, orchards, and well-tended fields fell to ruin as the countryside was developed. The typical suburban dwelling, although blessed with land, sunlight, rainfall, and other resources, makes little connection to its environment for support.

The suburbs are largely uninhabited most of the day except for the workers who operate lawn mowers, weed whackers, and leaf blowers to maintain dominance over the local ecology. Nearly every requirement for living is trucked in from far away. Few of life's necessities—work, recreation, schooling, food, or even drinking water—are available without getting into a motor vehicle.

Suburban consumption of the productive agricultural resources around cities corresponded with a period of especially rapid change in the food sector. Energy use, food packaging, consolidation and concentration in food companies, and municipal solid waste all increased dramatically. No-deposit, no-return containers made it easier for dairies, breweries, and bottlers to displace local businesses with large, centralized processing plants. Pig farms were literally turned into landfills as use of nonrefillable containers and plastic

wrappings skyrocketed and as pig farms were subjected to increasing regulation.

Now, the mutual dependency between the cities and the land
around them is greatly diminished. Most suburbanites do still depend on their good-paying urban jobs. They also rely on the cities to
deal with (or at least contain) the problems of poverty, crime, and
the environmental disasters left behind by "runaway" manufactur-
ers. Suburbs around here still send their trash into the city for burning. Those people left in the city can depend on higher taxes, on
clogged interstate highways running right through their towns, on
fewer opportunities for employment, and on having to import most
of their food needs from farther away. Connecticut now imports 85
percent of its food from an average of more than thirteen hundred
miles away. In the inner city, convenience stores and fast-food out-
lets have replaced the supermarkets that earlier replaced many of the
neighborhood markets. (Agricultural and energy subsidies make
processed food seem very cheap, and drain resources away from the
cities.)

The Future: Fighting Back with Small Farms and School Gardens

The emerging vision of a more locally sufficient region offers the
greatest hope for reinvigorating both the cities and the surrounding
areas. As we begin to explore the possibilities of a local food system,
we also see the potential for addressing a variety of other serious local problems.

Around here, a movement toward local food production with
community gardens, farmers' markets, and small farms in the
shadow of the city occurred in the late 1970s in response to energy
crises and a growing awareness of important issues in our food system. Its momentum slowed down in the 1980s when, if it wasn't a

new condominium or office park, it wasn't worth considering. Many of those new buildings are still empty, but the local food pioneers of the 1970s, joined now by a younger generation, are building on the earlier work in varied and creative ways.

Each spring for twelve years some of our farm animals—pigs, chickens, goats, and ducks—have gone to New Haven to become part of a small organic farm in a park where high school students study ecology while tending the farm and raising food for the school picnic. The educational success and relevance of this project led to the formation of the New Haven Ecology Project, which started a summer program for at-risk ninth graders and is planning to build a high school that uses a farm as the context for learning in all subject areas.

In the last few years, school gardens have been popping up almost like weeds in cities like New Haven and Bridgeport and in the suburbs, too. Gardens are important learning environments that engage and excite children. The students we garden with in Bridgeport are a wonderfully diverse and energetic group. Many of them have strong connections to rural areas down south, in the Caribbean, and in Central America. The school garden affirms an important part of their heritage and taps into a wealth of the students' prior knowledge. This is exhilarating work that builds our hopes.

Two Community-Supported Agriculture (CSA) projects have grown up in the last decade in New Haven's suburbs. One CSA provides ninety families with vegetables all summer. They both connect farmers and eaters directly and are models of successful, small-scale local agriculture. Since these farms are organic and hand tended, they make good neighbors. Other suburban farmers, old and new, are creating sustaining connections with urban markets and consumers.

A new organic farmers' market in New Haven gives smaller-scale and urban growers a chance to sell directly to eaters. Some of the produce is grown by neighborhood residents in a rocky vacant lot near the market.

The New Haven Land Trust worked with urban farmers to develop a network of community gardens throughout the city, as well as providing the education needed for successful growing. Rainbow Recycling set up compost systems at many community gardens.

For over a decade, creating compost from urban waste has been a very successful part of my farming activities. With the help of pigs and chickens, food waste and leaves from the city become a valuable resource. Surplus compost is sold to city dwellers and suburbanites to enrich their gardens.

Many of the younger families in town are serious about eating from their backyard and community gardens. A growing number keep a small flock of chickens right in the city. There's a resurgence in the use of wood, a renewable resource, to heat renovated and insulated urban dwellings.

My sense is that the move toward local sufficiency is happening in cities all over the country.

From what I understand of the big picture, if we don't work quickly to make the cities, the country, and the suburbs more nourishing, sustainable, and sufficient for our needs, we won't be around much longer. It's exciting work, and with the enthusiasm of children, the bounty of green plants, and nature's cycles on our side, we all just might be able to do it.

Seeking Knowledge and Wisdom

Some people look at Plain *and ask where the religion is. Where are the Scripture readings, sermons, God-talk in all this concern for living simply? What do essays on bike riding and farming have to do with ultimate questions like salvation and damnation?*

Others have figured out that the editor of Plain *considers clothes washing to be a sacred activity. If the Spirit of God is present in all that we do, then religious symbols and icons tend to fall away. The lowliest object, a wooden yarn spool turned on a hand lathe a century ago by an anonymous Shaker brother, is apprehended then as a religious artifact.*

Note the everydayness of Amish and Quaker life, the concern for practicality, simpleness, patient hard work, and you are well on the way to solving the riddle of this book, the riddle of What Really Matters.

" 'What matters?' is plainly and simply a religious question," *John Taylor Gatto tells us in this last section of* The Plain Reader. *Applying the love of God to daily life, minute by minute, is the answer. This involves responsibility, caring, and unconditional love. To practice love requires intimate knowledge of every person and situation we encounter.*

And so, we become seekers of knowledge, as opposed to mere sifters of information. We aren't mining data looking for some advantage over our competitors. Within the context of living out Christ's love

(What Matters), we want to know what works. The Plain Reader *offers some examples of practical knowledge to remind you that it still exists. Knowledge, love's practical side, whether it is global, local, practical, or spiritual, is the raw material of wisdom. May you receive some of the necessary learning here.*

Toys Really Are Us

JANE MARTIN

I was talking to my ten-year-old friend Rebecca.

"I'm writing about toys and what little children need."

"They just need to be loved and held."

"Yes, I agree! But that won't come out to four hundred fifty words."

"Okay, so say they really, really, really, really . . . need to be loved and held."

I asked my two-year-old daughter, Sarah, "What's your favorite toy?"

"Daddy."

The next day I asked Julia, my seven-year-old, "What's your favorite toy?"

"Sarah."

Being that I'm in the toy-selling business, this wasn't working out too well.

But alas, it's the truth. Toys are very nice, but hardly a necessity. However, parents really enjoy giving their kids toys, so let's discuss toys. How do we determine what toys are best for our children?

Imagine a field of wildflowers on a beautiful summer day, a blue sky, a slight breeze. Now what else belongs in this scene? A happy running child, of course! The field and the child both vibrate on the same frequency—free, natural, happy, uncomplicated, *alive*! Okay, now picture the same field, but this time add a TV set. No, no, not quite right. How about a brightly colored Mattel See 'N Say toy? Naaah! Barney? A Barbie doll? Sorry—they just don't make it.

This is how I feel about my kids' toys: They should be made of wood, cotton, silk, or wool; elements that belong in a child's world, that will connect quietly with their bodies, minds, and souls, and interact, back and forth, in that process we call learning. In my view, plastics, synthetic loud colors, brash sounds, and foreign-feeling synthetic fibers are out of place in a child's world, just like a TV set in that field of flowers.

After ten years of raising kids I've come to realize that they just naturally gravitate toward what they need. So now I let them lead me; then, I provide the appropriate tools they need. What they do certainly wouldn't fit into some preprogrammed curriculum designed to forcibly educate them. My son David spends hours seemingly doing nothing. But I realized one morning when he was six that what may look like nothing to me is actually very active for him.

Me, bellowing: *"David, wake up out of your daze and put on your shoes!!* We're late and you've been sitting there doing nothing for fifteen minutes."

David: "Mom, what's three-fourths plus seven-eighths?"

So the first thing is to get a sense of what's going on inside your child. Is she drawing trees everywhere? A set of block beeswax crayons and a three-foot-high pile of scrap paper from the office will mean more to her than the entire one-thousand-square-foot art aisle in Toys "R" Us. How many hours would your little boy spend outside with a simple ball? Sarah spent three hours a day for two weeks sitting in a sink full of water playing with my pots and pans; and how efficient—her toys could double as cooking utensils for me! Then she became a puzzle doer. And David all of a sudden fell in love with the solar system. You never know what will be next.

By far the most popular toy in our house is a basket of different colored silks. Any lightweight cloth will do. With a silk and a touch of imagination you can become anything! Many elaborate puppet shows have been created on a row of kitchen chairs draped with silks (yellow for the sun, black for night, green for the pasture and blue for the river). Complicated modern toys come with the story built in, but after two or three uses they become boring and end up sitting on a shelf. Children have incredible imaginations, and they need very little to let that come out. A good toy will act synergistically with the imagination.

In the same vein, a doll shouldn't dictate to the child. If a doll is simple in form and facial expression, the child will imagine the smile or the cry. A soft cotton body stuffed with wool is perfect for a young child. Square scraps from your sewing box can serve as bedding and provide many hours of folding—an activity toddlers love!

Boys (I know this is sexist, but it's what I've observed) just love trucks. Dump trucks that really work are best. Think about it—what seems more pleasant, a clanky-sounding, cold, metal (or plastic), brightly painted and decaled truck with gadgets that break off, or a wooden truck, simple in form and warm to the touch? And when the wooden truck breaks, bring out your Elmer's glue.

When choosing toys I always look for simple beauty. Wooden puzzles with whole, not cut-up, images. Wooden or cotton rattles that make earthy sounds. Wooden shovels and buckets that will look at home in the sand. If Mickey Mouse is not beautiful to you, then why assume it will be beautiful to your child?

I've concluded that Rebecca is right; a child needs little more than warm loving arms. How Toys "R" Us can fill thirty thousand square feet full of toys is beyond me. When a pile of rocks is so interesting to a toddler, when sliding on the snow or making a house out of tree limbs is such wonderful fun for the elementary school kids, when a shovel and sand provide an afternoon of play, and when helping Mom sweep is a four-year-old's favorite activity—how can we need thirty thousand square feet of toys? I say, keep your money, and your child might be better off!

Unless Ye Become As Little Children

GENE LOGSDON

My grandson Evan and I are walking up the woodlot lane from our house to the barn. He is two years old and I must walk slowly so as not to get ahead of him. In fact, I often follow him— which is almost the whole point of writing this. I let him wander along as he pleases. Being slower of step and closer to the ground, and equipped with a mind far less crowded with useless facts than I, he notices and appreciates more than I do.

"Pawpaw. See. 'Pider web." He squats and stares at the silky threads on the side of a stump. I point out the tunnel of web leading off to one side, where the spider is lurking.

He does not seem to pay attention, but next day, he takes Mawmaw up the path and points out to her where the spider "urks."

"Pawpaw. See. Hickee nut." He picks up the nut, knowing that when we get to the barn I will crack it with a hammer and we can see if its kernel is good or if it has been eaten by a wiggly white "orm."

A crow caws from somewhere in the treetops. "Pawpaw. Crow. Crow bird." And I congratulate him enthusiastically for remembering what he had only learned yesterday.

And so we proceed, foot by foot, a marvel waiting for him at every step. Recalling a statistic I read recently, that a child learns more in his first four years of life than he does in all the rest, I have to keep reminding myself of how almost everything is new to him, and how his mind must deal with a surge of experiences washing over it every moment that at a more advanced age would befuddle an Einstein.

When he was not much over one year old, he started his education, with no urging from me. At the hum of a plane, or distant tractor, or truck on the highway, he would tense in my arms, hold up a finger, and ask, "Dat?" At first I did not catch on, since I was so used to hearing the noises he was referring to that they hardly registered in my consciousness. But eventually he taught me to listen again. Then the conversation would go like this:

"Dat?" (for "what's that?") said tensely, because the human mind is fearful of what it does not comprehend.

"Truck," I'd answer.

"Comin'?" Still apprehensive, he was fearful of piston engine noises, so foreign to biological life and, indeed, so worthy of fear.

"No. Not coming. It's going on down the road," I'd say reassuringly. Then I'd add a lie. "It can't hurt you."

The retentiveness of a child's mind is amazing. "Haymow" comes out "haymouse" when Evan says it, but I needed to tell him that word only twice before he remembered it. The same with hay rake, haystack, mower, cow, calf, sheep, chicken, rooster, frog, toad, fish, grasshopper, worm, butterfly, tractor, rock, truck, airplane, and a hundred other things we come across in our play and work. He even quickly understood that "cat" and "Ginger," the name of our cat, stand for the same thing. And that birds are birds but may also be robins, blue jays, crows, etc. In other words, even at age two, children begin to master the sophisticated mental gymnastics of abstraction. When Evan keeps repeating a phrase such as "Go haymouse, Pawpaw; go haymouse, Pawpaw," I used to think he was nagging me to take him there, even though he knew I had already agreed to do so. But now I believe he was just practicing the word—to commit it to memory. And thrilled that he could say one more phrase that Pawpaw understood.

Carol and I "raised" our own two children and they have turned out to be wonderful people. Now we are helping "raise" our grandchildren. But I make no claims to knowing how to do this. Every child is different. And I am uncomfortable with the word "raise." It implies a controlling influence over children that I doubt adults really can exercise or at least are entitled to exercise. I fear this "raising" of children turns too often into squelching their true selves or their creative thinking in favor of someone else's notions. How often in "raising" children, do we merely transfer on to another generation our own biases about the truth, while any new idea occurring to a child's mind unencumbered by societal influence, we discourage before it can be profitably examined?

Children must be controlled and trained and disciplined, for sure. They are not little angels. But I wonder if we should not also heed the wisdom of the ages in "raising" them: virtue is moderation in all things. Evil, in my view, comes from an excessive desire to control other people.

According to the not-so-hidden agenda of public schools, children must be freed of the "bondage" of overly dominating religious belief, in favor of more liberating, scientific, objective views on life. There was a time when, as a teacher, I agreed with that agenda, at least a little. But "objective," scientific, nonreligious education has become overly dominating indoctrination into the religion of the State, where virtue is an unquestioning adoration of the god Money and submission to whatever the Moneygod's scientists-disciples-bureaucrats say is the truth as of this moment.

Unfortunately, excessive domination is exercised in private schools and private families, too. If we really love our children, we must be aware of the inclination for control in all of us, and humbly remember that none of us knows the whole truth. I am afraid that many modern parents are regimenting little children too much for the convenience of adults and out of ambition to make children into sports stars and millionaires and other myopic notions of success. I fear this regimentation mostly because it kills creativity—thinking for oneself—which in turn kills true leadership in a democracy and encourages sheeplike docility to totalitarian authority.

Electronic learning for children, even "good" electronic information like the compact-disc encyclopedias for computers and the nature programs on TV, is not a substitute for real-life experiences. The information stored electronically suffers all the faults of our other schooling tools, including the classroom itself. The information superhighway and the classroom are both artificial environments. Both are handy for teaching reductionist science that is based on the myth that if we measure and name all the parts of a thing, say a frog, then we understand frogs—when in fact we have only labeled frog parts. Look where reductionist science has led us: a world the poet Gary Snyder describes in his recent book, *A Place in Space,* as "a planet that was supposed to take us somewhere but which is now exploding in our hands."

Suppose your child wants some information on the bluebird. A knowledgeable teacher in a classroom might be able to supply some information. Or the child can easily be taught to punch up an encyclopedia program in a computer and not only get a brief natural history of the bird, but see it in fairly accurate colors and hear its song, too. That kind of knowledge, while instructive up to a point, is only reductive scientific description. Knowledge about bluebirds after looking at the best compact-disc encyclopedia is terribly fragmented, terribly oversimplified, and has the bad effect of inducing humans to believe that they are being sufficiently informed or "educated" about bluebirds.

A preoccupation with this sort of knowing explains why it has been so difficult for our society to appreciate ecology, the relationship between living things. Ecology is hardly able to be encompassed by "facts"; its understanding requires a kind of love that is foreign to "objective" reductionist science.

The computer program suffers another fault: time is the all-controlling consideration. An electronic encyclopedia that tried to give us all the known "facts" about bluebirds and their relationships with the whole ecology would cost a fortune and still fail. Likewise, nature programs on TV, however well executed technologically and narratively, must conform to strict time limits.

Mastering computer skills in the primary grades is just another way of pushing children too soon into adulthood. I recently heard a politician declare, as if no one could possibly disagree, that "we must introduce even young children into the computer age" as a first step to improving education. Pure rot. Millions and millions of people who lived through childhood before the computer existed have successfully mastered the machine. Even the people who invented computers lived through childhood before the machines existed!

Schoolchildren are now learning to operate computers and software that will most certainly be obsolete by the time the youngsters reach college, and they will have to learn all over again on something new. At best, children are being trained to be computer stenographers, a job that will, with the advent of voice-activated computers, also become obsolete.

There is risk involved in granting freedom to children. I used to feel uncomfortable when I saw a row of young Amish boys about twelve years old sitting in front of the supermarket in Kidron, Ohio, puffing away proudly on cigarettes. Their parents made no effort to stop them other than the gentle persuasion of example and a silent show of displeasure. But long experience has now taught me that such persuasion is the only effective response to teenage rebellion, as long as it follows many loving hours spent with the teens when they were younger. The Amish do not even require their children to commit to the Amish religion until the children have reached a more rational age and are convinced that they are ready to do so.

It is those earlier years, especially from about two to about nine, that are so important as to what follows. American parents seem bent on giving their children this age over to a life continuously regimented by adult ambition.

The aim seems to be to push even very young children into competition for future success (even though the parents don't know what kind of world the child will live in as an adult), rather than giving them ample time just to laugh, play, and dream, and to learn by the native curiosity of the mind.

It is impossible for the human mind not to learn, not to want to learn, not to be learning all the time. Schools don't want to admit that; they want parents to think learning is what takes place in classrooms.

To counter methods of controlled domination, I think people need to remember the biblical admonition: unless you become as little children you shall not enter the kingdom of heaven. In other words, we should start realizing that a simple, undisturbed, relatively unregimented life is good not only for children, but for adults, too. So many adults are restless, dissatisfied, and confused because they have lost the power to think for themselves enough even to understand the stupidity of life in a culture of socialized materialism.

I think (I truly do) that formal schooling of children as now constituted ought to be abolished at least until the age of ten. If children have to be grouped at all, let it be in small groups of no more than four to six people and then only for a few hours at a time. Regimentation is only necessary in large groups. Herding children together in such a way so that parents can work at some job is the most terrible mistake of modern times, in my opinion.

Herding does not develop good social attitudes toward others, as the champions of contemporary schooling maintain. It just as often encourages hostility, as we see all around us today. When people are more isolated, with more time alone or in very small groups, they are inclined to treat the larger world of people more kindly. Crowded together, people do just what rats do: they start killing each other. Children raised with an optimum amount of quiet time will not congregate at rock concerts or sports events in which they play no direct part and scream and stomp in ludicrous animal ecstasy of thought-obliterating noise.

The screamers and stompers are trying vainly to find some individual worth in the pulsations of the mob. They are prime candidates for despots to whip into frenzies of fake patriotism and for large corporations to herd into computer sweatshops. Groupieness, the hallmark of modern culture, drives out thought, and with it the impulse to stand against herd approval, which too often means herd-approved vice, as well. Groupieness is the enemy of democracy.

One of my heroes is the early-nineteenth-century farmer and writer William Cobbett, who all his life opposed the excesses of industrialism in England and predicted accurately that the mass migration of people from the rural, decentralized, pastoral economy to the urban, consolidated, factory economy would be England's eventual downfall. He supported the Luddites with his pen and spent time in jail for doing so. In one of his books, *Rural Rides,* he described as an aside how he educated his children without benefit of formal schooling. He went into detail about how he taught his son arithmetic by actually using it in the daily work of the farm, and how easily his son picked up ciphering in this way. In those days, formal schooling often used the birch rod to enforce learning, and Cobbett was particularly scathing in his criticism of that practice. Here are some wonderful quotes about Industrial Age education two centuries ago, which the schooling fraternity still doesn't get:

Now when there is much talk about education, let me ask you how much money it generally costs parents to have a boy taught arithmetic; how much time it costs also; and . . . how much mortification . . . it costs the poor scolded, brokenhearted child, who becomes dunder-headed and dull for all his lifetime, merely because that has been imposed on him as a task which he ought to regard as a pleasant pursuit . . .

And again:

I never yet saw in my house a child that was afraid; that was in any fear whatever; that was ever for a moment under any sort of apprehension, on account of the learning of anything; and I never in my life gave a command, an order, a request, or even advice, to look into any book; and I am quite satisfied that the way to make children dunces, to make them detest books, and justify that detestation, is to tease them and bother them about the subject. . . . I am sure, from thousands of instances that have come under my own eyes, that to begin to teach children book-learning before they are capable of reasoning is the sure and certain way to enfeeble their minds for life; and if they have natural genius, to harm, if not totally destroy, that genius.

To counter the deadly hand of organized learning, here are some suggestions:

1. Provide quiet time in your life, as in your child's life. Some solitude is good for the soul and I believe essential to sanity. So is time spent in the intimacy of a very small group, as with just two people exchanging ideas. I don't think you can achieve this goal by scheduling "quality time" with a child, either. That is just another form of regimentation. The child who merely plays at her mother's feet while Mother works in the kitchen experiences real quality time. Both mother and child are sharing something precious: being

alone together, enjoying a silence not needing to be broken, immersed in that wonderful unconscious feeling that "all's right in the world."

2. Let learning proceed creatively in children, and in yourself, from natural curiosity without thought as to whether the knowledge gained be of money-usefulness or whether it jibes with somebody's "lesson plan." Children, with their as yet uncrowded minds, are particularly receptive to creative, imaginative learning.

Evan delights in my "crazy" implausible stories because in very short order he understands that I am revealing something wondrous about the real world when I tell them. Like most small children, he will pick up on make-believe instantly, and very shortly add his own make-believe to mine, and we both therefore derive new ways to think about the real world. Our relationship is not teacher-student but two people joyfully learning as equals.

3. When a child does ask you questions, resist the temptation to go into a formal teaching mode. Don't try to make a profound lesson out of everything that occurs in the child's daily life. Don't always be correcting a child for simple mistakes. Don't lecture them (or adults, either, as I am doing). The terrible compunction parents and teachers feel to cram information into little children's minds in nursery school, preschool, kindergarten, and the primary grades is a madness. The madness is prompted by a perceived need to make sure the student passes standardized tests. The madness also infests parents who think they must push the child along to "success" right from birth, lest the poor thing not get into a "good" college.

4. Do nothing. Small children know only the moment. They don't anticipate the future very much, even the future an hour from now. Things just happen as they crawl or tumble around, and everything that happens is momentous to them.

As they grow into adulthood, they get caught up in the anticipation of future events (which seldom live up to their expectations)

and so ignore the thousand little marvels of the moment around them. A good example of this oversight is the throng of people in our town who ignore the exceptional beauty of autumn trees along their streets, and drive with the herd four hundred miles to look at fall colors in a national park.

5. Do not routinely insert electronic machines between children and real life, and think that by so doing you are educating them. While technology and schooling train people to program and operate computers, who is worrying about where the talent will come from that creates worthwhile thoughts to fill the computer with? A computer can, perhaps, store the world's wisdom, but it can never produce that wisdom.

We are building an information superhighway while the journey of creative human thought travels a lonely country lane.

What Really Matters

John Taylor Gatto

G oing to the moon didn't really matter, it turned out.
I say that from the vantage point of my six decades living on
Planet Earth but also because of something I saw not so long ago.
It was at Booker T. Washington High School where I watched an
official astronaut, a handsome, well-built black man in his prime,
dressed in a silver spacesuit, with an air of authentic command, try
to get the attention of an auditorium full of Harlem teenagers. It
was the board of education's perfect template for dramatic success—
a distinguished black man leading ignorant black kids to wisdom.
He came with every tricky device and visual aid NASA could
muster, yet the young audience ignored him completely. At several
places in his presentation he couldn't continue for the noise. Maybe
the kids instinctively perceived this astronaut had less control over
his rocket vehicle than a bus driver has over his bus. It's even possible they had also wordlessly deduced that any experiments he performed were someone else's idea. NASA. The space agency's hype
was lost on them.

This man for all his excellence was only some other man's *agent*.
I think the kids sensed that his talk, too, had been written by someone else. He was part of what the Protestant theologian Reinhold
Niebuhr called the "non-thought" of received ideas. It was irrele-
vant whether this astronaut understood the significance of his ex-

periments or not. He was only an agent, not a principal—in the same way many schoolteachers are only agents retailing someone else's orders. This astronaut wasn't walking his own talk but some-one else's. A machine can do that.

It seems likely that my Harlem kids considered going to the moon a dumb game; obviously I didn't verify their feelings scientifi-cally but I knew a lot of them didn't have fathers or much dignity in their lives, and about half had never eaten off a tablecloth. What was going to the moon supposed to mean to them? If you asked *me* that question, I couldn't answer it with any confidence, and I *had* a father once upon a time . . . and a tablecloth, too.

A lot of things don't matter that are supposed to; one of them is well-funded government schools. Saying that may be considered ir-responsible by people who don't know the difference between schooling and education, I know, but over one hundred academic studies have tried to show any compelling connection between money and learning and not one has succeeded. Right from the be-ginning, schoolmen told us that money would buy results and we all believed it. So, between 1960 and 1992 the U.S. tripled the number of constant dollars given to schools. Yet after twelve thousand hours of government schooling, one out of five Americans can't read the directions on a medicine bottle.

After twelve thousand hours of compulsory training at the hands of nearly one hundred government-certified men and women, many high school graduates have no skills to trade for an income or even any skills with which to talk to each other. They can't change a flat, read a book, repair a faucet, calculate a batting average, install a light, follow directions for the use of a word processor, build a wall, make change reliably, be alone with themselves, or keep their marriages together. The situation is considerably worse than journalists have discerned. I know, because I lived in it for thirty years as a teacher.

Last year at Southern Illinois University I gave a workshop in what the basic skills of a good life are as I understand them. Toward the end of it a young man rose in back and shouted at me, "I'm twenty-five years old, I've lived a quarter of a century, and I don't know how to do anything except pass tests. If the fan belt on my car broke on a lonely road in a snowstorm, I'd freeze to death. Why have you done this to me?"

He was right. I was the one who did it, just as much as any other teacher who takes up the time young people need to find out what really matters. I did it innocently and desperately, trying to make a living and keep my dignity, but nevertheless I did it by being an agent of a system whose purpose has little to do with what kids need to grow up right. My critic had two college degrees, it turned out, and his two degrees were shrieking at me that going to school doesn't matter very much even if it gets you a good job. People who do very well in schools as we've conceived them have much more than their share of suicides, bad marriages, family problems, unstable friendships, feelings of meaninglessness, addictions, failures, heart bypasses that don't work, and general bad health. These things are very well documented, but most of us can intuit them without any need for verification. If school is something that *hurts* you, what on earth are we allowing it for?

Does going to school *matter* if it uses up all the time you need to learn to build a house? If a fifteen-year-old kid was allowed to go to the Shelter Institute in Bath, Maine, he would be taught to build a beautiful post-and-beam Cape Cod home in three weeks, with all the math and calculations that entails; and if he stayed another three weeks, he'd learn how to install a sewer system, water, heat, and electric. If any American dream is universal, owning a home is it; but few government schools bother teaching you how to build one. Why is that? Everyone thinks a home matters.

Does going to school matter if it uses up the time you need to start a business, to learn to grow vegetables, to explore the world, or to make a dress? Or if it takes away time to love your family? What matters in a good life?

The things that matter in a *bad* life, we know, are: gaining power over others, accumulating as much stuff as you can, getting revenge on your enemies (who are everywhere), and drugging yourself one way or another to forget the pain of not quite being human. School teaches most kids how to strive for a bad life and succeeds at this so well that most of our government machinery eventually falls into the hands of people who themselves are living bad lives. We're all in deep trouble because of that. It's the best reason I know to keep the machinery of government just as weak and as primitive as possible as soon as we figure out how.

It surprises me how many graduates leave college assuming they know what matters because they got straight As. If we can believe advertisements, what matters to these people most is the personal ownership of machinery: blending machines, cooking machines, driving machines, picture machines, sound machines, toothbrushing machines, computing machines, machines to kill insects, deliver intimacy, send messages through wires or the naked air, entertainment machines, shooting machines, and many more mechanical extensions of our physical self. Indirect control over even more ambitious machines seems to matter a lot, too: flying machines, bombing machines, heart and lung machines, voting machines, and a great variety of other mechanical creations.

All these devices are meant to defeat what otherwise would occur naturally if they didn't exist. They are all machines to beat human destiny and confer on human beings magical powers and the reach and longevity of gods.

Do they deliver what they promise? Is human life in a net sense better since their advent? I can't answer that for you, of course, but you can look into your heart and answer the question for yourself. Someone has apparently convinced us that what occurs naturally cannot be the way to a good life, hence these battalions of machinery. What percentage of your life is spent talking to machines, buying them, mastering them, ministering to their needs, then betraying them with ever newer and newer machine loves? It takes a lot of time, but what does it take a lot of time away from? Television has cost the average twenty-one-year-old about eighteen thousand hours of time. What would that time have gone toward otherwise? Learning to build a house? Going to government-run school takes another fifteen thousand hours from the young life, twenty-one thousand if you count going and coming and homework. What might this time have gone toward otherwise? From the very small amount of time remaining, machinery other than television gobbles a great deal. What does it give back in return? Heartsease? Love? Courage? Self-reliance? Friends? Dreams?

Here we are, at the end of the twentieth century, well machined yet lost in a tunnel of loneliness, cut off from each other, disliking ourselves, envying those with superior machines, looking for self-respect and significance. We have fewer and worse human ties than seems possible if machines justified all the time and money spent on them. I include, of course, the social machinery of school in this critique. From age five, when we go to school, to age twenty-one there are exactly 140,160 hours. We spend 46,720 of them in sleep, and of the remaining 93,000-odd hours, 42 percent are spent *watching* TV from a chair or *sitting* in a school seat. Something is wrong here. What is going on? How much do these seemingly essential machines matter? What are they essential for? Each one taken separately can easily be justified, but taken all together, what are they doing to us?

By midcentury we had reached a point in this machine civilization where we could so little bear intimate contact with the messy reality of living things—as compared to the clean simplicity of machines—that we became willing to lock up our mothers and fathers wholesale. To create a new investment opportunity in warehousing the old. What a strange thing to do with our unprecedented wealth, using it, that is, to divest ourselves of our closest human ties, getting rid of our history. In doing so a complex circle begun a century earlier when we first locked our young people away in school warehouses was completed. Warehousing the young, warehousing the aged—good business, I know, but good for what?

Does it really matter or not that our parents die among strangers and our children live penned up by strangers? Does that possibly have an effect on the quality of the lives neither old nor young who are left theoretically "free" of entanglements? Entanglements are, after all, the core of complete human lives; good lives are all about being entangled with each other. The assertion that isolation chambers for the young and old are an advance in human society doesn't square with any observable reality; it, too, is part of the great nonthought of received ideas—like pretending a positive significance to the idiotic space program.

After you fall into a habit of accepting what other people tell you to think, you lose the power to think for yourself. I suspect that's why so few of us challenge the premises of old-age homes, television, day-care centers, and schools.

Talking to machines as we have come to prefer to do does make us intimate with the way machines think; it also conceals from us the degree to which our own lives are mechanical and our own thoughts well-controlled like the thoughts of machinery. Have you noticed that machines don't ever surprise you after you know their habits? The purpose of market research is to remove surprise from human behavior, too. When we lose the power to surprise each other, we lose a chunk of what it means to be human. Would that matter?

I want to argue that talking to machines when you should be talking to people and the natural world is what has clear-cut the Pacific forests, poisoned the fish in Puget Sound, weakened the soil up and down America, turned Cape Cod Bay into a dead sea, and burned holes in the stratosphere. Not a single one of those events would matter at all to machinery, and since machinery is what we have been most intimate with since early childhood (including social mechanisms like government schools), they don't matter to us, either, regardless of what we say. If they mattered, we would stop it.

At best we're ambivalent. Who in his right mind would live without an automobile, a computer, a fax machine, a telephone, a toaster, lifelong schooling, or a gun? Everyone who winds life around a core of machinery—physical machinery or social machinery, like schools and institutions and global corporations—is affected profoundly, and comes inexorably, I believe, to be a servomechanism of the machinery he or she excessively associates with.

So far I've asked you to consider three aspects of modern American life we all have been accustomed to think really matter: the space program, our well-funded government schooling, and state-of-the-art technology. On close inspection all seem to me the obsessions of madmen more than essential parts of a good life or a good society. How did they come to matter when many things that *really* matter (like getting hugged a lot) are overlooked?

In recent years I've often heard that what really matters most is competing successfully in something called the global economy. Try to pass over the fact that all economies on earth, every single one of them including Japan's, are overwhelmingly *national* economies, or that the economies that seem to make people happiest and proudest are substantially *local* ones, and look at what you are being asked to believe. In effect, it is claimed that America's total self-sufficiency in food doesn't matter, that our embarrassing abundance of many fuels, fibers, metals, building materials, roads, technologies, libraries, colleges, and talented labor no longer matters decisively, because in some mysterious way we stand in grave danger of losing these things by becoming globally noncompetitive. I will pass over the fact that with a standing army, navy, and air force of over two and a half million men and women, a vast bombing fleet, an enormous arsenal of nuclear missiles, and a worldwide network of spies and saboteurs, it is really impossible to be noncompetitive; and I will pass over our vast ability to manipulate money markets and currencies, which makes being noncompetitive quite unlikely for all the foreseeable future.

But I am puzzled by the rhetoric of global competition, because we already possess abundantly all the essentials of a good material life, "in-house" as it were. What will this global economy exist *for* if not to produce and distribute more material, develop more skill, more jobs, and more satisfaction—things out of which good lives are made? But these things are already here. I'm curious about the kind of human being who thinks this global economy matters, because it's clear to me they are caught up in a religious vision, a rather peculiar one in which human nature is disregarded along with the human needs that really matter—all of which needs are overwhelmingly small scale.

It's easy to see how a global economy would matter to the spirit of mass-production machinery or to international banking, with all the urgencies of those twin mechanisms, but not so clear what the point of it is for flesh and blood.

What if you forgot all about the globe and concentrated instead on finding a place where you could feel at home for the rest of your life? What if you shaped your own work so that it served your spirit and the spirits of your loved ones, friends, and neighbors? In 1776 a full 90 percent of Americans not in slavery shaped their own work, they had independent livelihoods, and in 1840, despite the rise of in-dustrialization the figure was still 80 percent. It was hard then for any man to get rich on the labors of others because there wasn't much free-floating labor to be had; people worked for themselves. *That*—liberty and independence, *not* wealth or comfort—was the American miracle.

You know, machines can be stored anywhere, can function any-where, and are indifferent to other machines they must associate with. But men and women have to build the meanings of their lives around a few people, a very few people to touch and love and care for. If you're always getting rid of people, trading them off the way you've been taught to trade off things, you can't have much of a life. And if you fail in this vital endeavor of linking up with the right people for you, it doesn't matter at all how healthy the space pro-gram is or how many machines you own. You'll still be lonely in the middle of crowds.

If what I've said is even partly true, you'll have to join me in sabotaging the global economy and sabotaging the government schools, because schools and government and machinery makers lie to you about what matters every time. They just can't help themselves.

Whatever you think about all this, the question "What matters?" can't be avoided. If you follow the path of experts in this, you'll be in for a series of unpleasant shocks as you discover by living that experts are almost always incomplete people who don't quite know what matters.

"What matters?" is plainly and simply a religious question, and machines and experts know nothing at all about such things. Nor do societies that pattern their workings after the logic of machinery—as our own has done since the advent of universal compulsory schooling at the turn of the twentieth century. In those same formative years the U.S. Supreme Court amazed the world by declaring that corporations, those abstract legal machines, were actually living persons in the eyes of the law, enjoying all legal human rights that men and women did. You don't have to be a genius to see that when the Boss says a mere economic machine is really a Man, then it is only a little distance to discovering that a Man is really a Machine.

On the threshold of the twenty-first century you have to decide whether it matters or not to behave like a machine and take orders from a central planning agency. If it does matter and you vote against it, you face the difficult task of establishing what it costs to be completely human. In what way does such a condition obligate you? Might it suggest, for instance, that you accept the responsibility of caring for your own parents in their helplessness as they may have cared for you in yours? (Or caring for them even if they didn't care for you?) Machines would recognize no such obligations, of course.

It is painful, this thinking for yourself, but it forces you to be fully aware that being human means exercising free will. And the only way that happens is by making commitments and paying the heavy price for honoring them. Otherwise you are only a bit of machinery, your actions predestined by statistical market research, and that is true no matter how light and free you feel for the moment with a drink in your hand.

If you still believe that real meaning can be extracted from dramas of journalism like the space program or the latest word from Bosnia, you must end up addicted to strangely abstract urgencies, to causes, labels, slogans, and synthetic thrills, to dependency on checklists to organize your life. If you think life's meaning is determined by artificial associations like government schools, political parties, hospitals, corporations, or central planning agencies as John Dewey did, instead of by the change of seasons or a walk beside the ocean, you're bound to end up dumbed down (even if a PhD), sick (even if well medicated), and homeless (though your household be ever so scientifically constructed). And if you think you can safely talk to machines for very long, you will certainly go crazy doing it.

So figure out what matters. Relying on others in this regard will ruin you. Each of us has a design problem to solve: to create from the raw material around us the curriculum of a good life. It isn't easy to do, and it isn't the same puzzle for any two people. Real human beings are *particular* entities, regardless of how inconvenient that truth is for social scientists who love to talk of mass man. If you think you can buy such particularity, look around you at the shambles my own generation has made trying to buy it or fashion it with machinery.

Where to start? First you have to find yourself; there isn't any other way. If you wait for others to show you how, you'll wait till hell freezes over. You have to strip away decades of outside programming and overlays to discover your own outline beneath it all. It hurts to do that. This was once called "knowing" yourself. Schools are careful not to allow kids any privacy to do that, but until you take that step there won't be any self for you to know, just a collection of relays and switches manipulated by social engineers you can't see. On the other hand, when you do figure out what matters—and if you are willing to fight and even die for it—then you are truly free. Nobody will ever again be able to colonize your mind.

One important way men and women come to know themselves is to closely study their own families. People who run from that obligation will find no substitute for the missing knowledge. Cut off from the roots, their lives are a lifelong withering process regardless of how well they do at making money. The best justification for the expanding universe of home schooling is the laboratory of family it creates, in which coming to know yourself and your own people is the central theme behind all appearances. Another way we come to know ourselves is by introspectively studying our own affirmations and refusals. What do you reflexively choose to do? What do you reject? The data you need to analyze is written in your own history and actions, and the power to interpret it comes best out of solitudes and meditations. Voluntary solitudes lead to depth of intellect and character and depth of piety. When children daydream in school they are seeking this condition that schools hysterically deny. People who avoid solitude have a dependency disease that makes them dangerous to others, yet schools give regular training in avoiding solitude.

The most radical act of refusal you can make is in refusing to become a nonperson, as our technocratic society would have you be. Think of Mother Teresa, who refused to admit that she was old and ugly, poor and powerless. And in her refusal she forced the rest of us to acknowledge she wasn't any of those things. Acts of affirmation and acts of refusal always matter. Refuse people who beg you for help and you define the limits of your personal humanity, the line in you where flesh and blood give way to dead machinery. Extending your hand in acts of affirmation enlarges the human zone, forcing the machine in you to retreat.

Learn to forgive and you will enter an arena of spectacular affirmation. Begin by forgiving yourself, then forgive your family; in doing so you establish a foundation for self-respect and for categorical love. Categorical love, by the way, is the kind that isn't given or taken away by the logic of good performance; it is offered freely without any conditions. If you affirm forgiveness, you have discovered the secret of eternal renewal so clearly described in the Christian Gospels.

When you love people who hurt you, the effect is utterly transcendental. You swell up with a sense of full humanity, freed from the dead hand of getting even. My own family taught me how to do this; now forgiveness is one of the affirmations I struggle to practice. When I succeed I feel blessed.

To be real, you need, too, to celebrate your own history, humble and tormented as it might be. What does it matter what others think; it is yours. Wear it gladly. You need to celebrate the history of your own parents and grandparents, too, even if they weren't the nicest people. It is the clay out of which you sprang; reject it and you reject yourself. Only bad can come of that. Cherish what is yours. Protect it. Defend it. Never accept the evaluation of outsiders in regard to it. Whether your family is the best or the worst doesn't matter nearly as much as newspaper people and welfare officials tell us it does. Being first or last at anything truly matters very little.

Refuse to be trivialized by an economic order that assigns important work to people who hold academic titles like doctor of philosophy instead of allowing any man or woman who can do it to do it. Hold authorities who allow our forests to be clear-cut in contempt, not anger. Keeping score by income or status is the mark of a limited mind; past a point, your possessions and labels crush you under their weight, dictate your behavior, waste your time, dominate your human relationships. When that happens you slowly become a machine, however well fed and secure. Instead, affirm a world of moral seriousness where everyday things are sacred to you. When you can make that happen, even the leaves and grass sparkle and shine, lighting up the darkness.

Trust yourself. Reject the insane claims that technological progress is human progress. Such nonsense is equivalent to claiming human destiny and machine improvement are wrapped up together in some way. They are not. The spirit of machinery seeks to infect living things and make them like machinery, too; that is what, I think, lies at the bottom of the cynical global system of industrial development. Better to be John Henry than the steam hammer; better an outcast than a votary of the new world order. Learn to live free or you will never know life at all, and that, I can guarantee you, really does matter.

Reject people and institutions that teach you that nothing is sacred; their legacy has degraded our national culture. We live in history's wealthiest political state, which has been locked in a consumption trance for a hundred years, devouring its children, its families, its hills, sky, and water in order to buy machinery to talk to. The government schools have been the *church* where such training in continuous consumption occurs.

It's time to change that and begin to teach what really matters.

Deleting Childhood

MARY ANN LIESER

About a year ago, my family moved away from the home where we'd lived for three years, within the borders of a town with a very high median income. Most of my neighbors then had much more disposable income than I. Many of the local businesses thrive by catering to the interests of people who demand "nothing but the best" and are willing to pay for it.

The standard among my neighbors was for children to begin a formal preschool program at the age of two. Many local preschools advertised their programs by listing all the myriad "enrichment" activities offered, usually including (and highlighting) computer instruction. Around the corner and down the road from my house was a storefront business offering nothing but computer classes and individualized computer instruction for children, from toddlers to teenagers. These pay-by-the-hour classes were promoted locally with all the usual dire warnings: "Start them young or they'll be left hopelessly behind in the dazzling Information Age future they are destined to inherit."

Some parents, who might not otherwise have been drawn to provide computer instruction for their very young children, are led to enroll them because of these advertising campaigns and by peer pressure from other affluent adults. They reason that, if all the other four-year-olds know how to turn on the machine and make colors flash across the screen, maybe little Katie will be behind when she starts school. So off Katie goes to computer camp.

I'm worried about what Katie is missing, too, but I'm not worried that her computer skills will be forever lagging. I'm worried about what Katie (along with millions of other modern children) is missing because of all the things she's not doing during the hours she spends in front of a computer terminal. And I'm worried computer instruction, computer play, and educational computer drills at school and at home are affecting the way in which today's children will forever view the world and the other people who live in it.

They certainly won't be missing anything they can't easily catch up on in later years, even if parents and teachers were to delay all computer exposure until high school or beyond. After all, millions of adults who never saw a computer as children are currently making a living using computers, designing them, writing software for them. Many learned what they know now in a few years of intensive, hands-on experience. They didn't start at age two with *Sesame Street* software. And children today can catch up with high technology twenty years from now, if that's what they choose. We should be asking ourselves, What sort of things *can't* they catch up on twenty years from now, if they don't spend enough time doing them in the present?

Coloring, cutting and pasting, listening to nursery rhymes, building pretend houses out of sticks in the backyard, molding clay or beeswax or play dough between their hands, playing in the mud without concern for how dirty they might get, rolling in the grass, building with wooden blocks, watching ants and bees and grasshoppers, creating their own scripts for their own puppet shows, playing store with pretend food and money, making up silly songs and singing them, swinging, talking to dogs and cats and other animals, riding tricycles and scooters and all sorts of wheeled toys, climbing and jumping and running, listening to stories, building roads and tunnels and cities in a sandbox, listening to more stories and making up their own to tell, being children, discovering the world—the real world, with sounds and smells and tastes—at their own pace and in their own way. In short, all the elements that made up a typical early childhood for the generations who came before television and computers.

For thousands of years children have learned about the world through direct experience. It is evident now to many who study child development that children have an inherent ability to spontaneously seek out those experiences that will most challenge them and help them to grow at the times they are most ready for them, with very little outside guidance. Of course, children need lots of moral and spiritual guidance, and a good example set in the home. However, the practice of providing them with a mediated experience—computers and television—as a substantial part of how they learn about the world is an experiment to which I am unwilling to submit my own children.

Those who champion the use of computers with children generally believe that a computer is just another tool for us to use, another medium of information and communication. The introduction of computers to children is a good thing, they say, because it will enrich the child's world by broadening the child's horizons. The more varied the child's world, the better, they assert.

But I believe that computers are not just a tool we use for good or ill, as the case may be. Computers use us, too. A computer is not simply an addition to the real world, especially for children; it changes the way its user views the real world, even when the user is away from the screen. No matter how sophisticated the graphic capability or how flashy the program (and I realize that many are quite impressive these days), computers reduce everything that moves through them into raw bits of information, and thereby move us away from the subtle presencing of the real world into the grossness of a two-dimensional world that bears little resemblance to the beautiful creation that envelops us.

Just as the heavy user of fast-action video games becomes less able, over time, to attend to the extremely slow-action, real-time beauty of a sunset, I believe computer use renders us less able to see the subtle and many-dimensional beauty of our world.

I have noticed a commensurate and increasing move away from fine detail and toward a grosser level of perception in many of the artifacts with which our culture surrounds children. Several years ago my daughter participated in a week of preschool vacation bible school at a church near our home, and I assisted one of the adult organizers, a neighbor and friend of mine. I enjoyed getting to know the children, but was frustrated each day when it was time for them to color or draw a picture. There were almost no crayons to be found, but one of the other adults could always produce a canister full of color markers. Many of the children seemed to prefer using markers rather than crayons anyway. The colors were brighter and a larger space on the paper could be filled in less time. But they also almost always bled through the paper, making every child's picture a messy blob of dark color.

The next time I was at a store that carried such items, I looked for a large box of crayons to purchase. I finally did find what I wanted, but only after looking at box after box of markers. Color markers of every imaginable size and color had taken over what was formerly the crayon section, and they now occupied approximately five times as much shelf space as crayons.

So what's so wonderful about crayons, and what's so bad about markers?

Everything we give our children teaches them something. Crayons teach children that there is variety and subtlety in the world, and that little things matter. After much crayon use, a child discovers that it makes a difference how hard you press down, and in what direction your strokes go. Markers teach children that little things don't matter. Many different levels of pressure all produce the same shade on the paper.

Markers seem to me to be most appropriate for children who are accustomed to learning the concepts of "less" and "more" from public television's *Sesame Street*, rather than from being in the kitchen helping Mom, and who learn about colors on a computer screen, rather than by helping to sort the laundry. But I don't believe that markers are what children really need at all.

Computer advocates also tout the use of computers with very young children because of the independent learning children can conduct at a computer terminal. The child can gain a sense of mastery and control, they assert, by learning that predictable things will happen when particular buttons are pressed. Not only that, but the child is just as capable of pressing the button and controlling what happens on the screen as is an adult, who otherwise does so many things a child, to his or her frustration, cannot do.

This argument ignores the fact that what the child is gaining mastery over is a machine, hooked up to a power source. Shut off the power and the child controls nothing. What the child is controlling with a computer is a series of preselected, predigested choices. Granted, much of today's sophisticated computer software presents quite an array of choices, but all the possibilities have ultimately been decided by some other person or the machine itself.

Instead, I'm teaching my preschoolers mastery over paper, scissors, and glue. Combined with their own imagination, this sort of mastery will take them further than any computer software ever will, for there is no limit to what can be created with scissors, paper, and glue. My four-year-old daughter has made hats, baskets, quilts, wings, bulrushes (for a play she helped script), birthday cards, coats, capes, aprons, Indian headdresses, boats, leaves, hearts, and flowers, most of which have been entirely of her own design and execution.

A child can learn many things through the process of creating such an item: how to plan and carry out an idea; how to construct; how to problem-solve when something doesn't work out at first; and the sheer joy of finishing, and knowing you made, a thing that didn't exist before, and that is unique among all the other things in the world.

I believe it's important for children to learn all of this by using their own hands on three-dimensional, real-world items. Being "creative" by pushing plastic keys to select items in a computer program's menu cannot compare.

Introducing computers to young children also serves to accelerate the growing gap between young and old, already so large in our culture. I used to hear it all the time when I worked in a large, urban public library. Grandparents would come in and either shudder or run the other way in fear when they saw a computer. But at the same time they would brag about their grandchildren's facility with computers.

The younger generation, some of these elders seemed to believe, was in some mysterious way predisposed from birth to be comfortable with computers. Actually, most of the younger generation's comfort can be accounted for by exposure and familiarity, while the older generation's fear and distrust may be well placed.

The elderly are respected in many other cultures, precisely because of what they know—because of their wisdom and knowledge. In a culture that places no value on wisdom and knowledge, favoring (or even worshipping) information instead, the elderly are held in low esteem. What does Grandpa have to offer when he doesn't even care to learn how to turn on the computer, much less use it?

The answer is that a grandparent offers a base of experience that is large enough to make some sense of the "information" with which we all, especially our children, are burdened.

Computer use by children is being sold to us on the basis of its supposed ability to broaden experience. But what is being given up in return? Our children's relationships with their grandparents' generation, with those who sustain the link between past, present, and future, will be impossible to experience twenty years later, along with all the other dimensions and wonders that computers have begun to delete from childhood.

The Singing Place

GENE LOGSDON

Riley and Sooz had helped weed the garden rows with more alacrity than usual, because Grandmaw had promised to take them to the Singing Place along the creek if there were time afterward. Homeschooled in every sense of the word, the children found it hard to believe that anything as unusual as the Singing Place could exist in their neighborhood, their domain, their classroom, without their knowledge of it.

So now they walked with Grandmaw across the farm toward the creek, full of anticipation about what the Singing Place might look or sound like. That they were in for an adventure they were sure. They had long since grown accustomed to Grandmaw's genius for finding drama and excitement in what others thought of as the simple and commonplace. They thought all grandmaws were like that.

"See that patch of wild 'spar'gus," Riley, age eleven, pointed out to her. "There are twelve different patches on our farm, and eighty-four stalks altogether. We've already cut fifty-seven. Yum. I love 'spar'gus, 'specially with mushrooms. Daddy found a hundred and forty-five big yellows so far, but I didn't find a one."

Ten-year-old Sooz led Grandmaw by the hand to a hollow tree and pointed upward. "Old horned owl has two babies up there," she explained. "Sometimes they peek out of their nest. They are snow-white."

"They turn brown when they grow up," Riley added in his best big-brother manner.

"Just the opposite of Grandmaws," Grandmaw opined.

To all their shows-and-tells, she reacted as if she had just heard the most exciting news in the world, which, in her mind, was indeed the case. She understood that the world a person could actually see, smell, touch, taste, and hear—the local world of daily life—was the only place to learn anything deeply enough to approach true knowledge. Global thinking was the myth of electronics. Global thinking begot only half knowledge that was worse than ignorance.

"Yesterday, mother owl fed a rabbit to her babies," Sooz said. "Poor little rabbit!"

"That's what rabbits are for," Grandmaw replied. "If we all don't eat each other, we're all goners. Death is the beginning of life."

If the children recognized any significance in Grandmaw's words, they did not say so. Nor did Grandmaw press the point. All in good time.

"There are five hundred and forty-two trees in this woods," Riley, the numberer, the scientist, announced. "Not counting the little ones."

"I expect they are mostly hickories like that one," Grandmaw said, trying to keep her face expressionless.

"Grandmaw, that's not a hickory, that's an ash," Riley replied with the gentle exasperation of a teacher correcting a child.

"Do tell," the old woman replied in a pretended huff that belied the satisfaction spreading over her countenance. Her grandchildren already knew more about the real world than most high school graduates do. "And I suppose you're going to try to tell me that one over there is a white oak."

"Nope," said Sooz. "It's a red oak. Leaves are pointed, not rounded."

"Well, if you're so smart, what's that little frowsy thing over there with all the white blossoms?"

Neither child knew.

"I don't know either," Grandmaw said. "What shall we call it?"

"Let's call it No-Name," said Sooz.

"Good as any," Grandmaw concurred. "Half of what passes for education is just names of things. Doesn't mean you know anything just because you know the names. We'll have to watch now and see what comes from those blossoms."

By this time, the trio had reached the creek. The children, full of expectation, watched Grandmaw closely as she picked her way carefully along the bank. Finally she stopped, gazed upstream and down, a perplexed look on her face.

"It's gone," she finally said. "Floodwaters must have washed away the Singing Place."

"Grandmaw, what do you mean?" Sooz asked, full of wonder and impatience together.

"It was right here," the old woman went on. "A bunch of rocks in the creek there where the current speeds up below that quieter pool. The rocks made a chain of little waterfalls and rapids. The water splashed and bubbled and gurgled and made music over the rocks. That's why when I was your age I called it the Singing Place."

All three stared disappointedly at the quiet-flowing stream. Grandmaw suddenly snapped her fingers. "Tell you what. We'll make the crick sing again."

And with that she took off her boots and socks, rolled up her pants and shirtsleeves, and began carrying rocks from the banks and creek bed, plopping them into the fast current. Shortly, she created a little rapids and a watery chatter of splashing and gurgling sounds.

"Now there," she said. "You can hear the music begin. All we need is more rocks to get a whole symphony going. A few violins here, a trombone and flute over there, and maybe a pie-ano yonder."

The children grasped the possibilities instantly. They began to gather rocks and place them into the creek bed, too, with indeed a more studied gravity than Grandmaw, as if they were professional creek music makers.

"Okay, Grandmaw, listen close," Riley commanded. "Which sound do you like better: if I place this green rock right here and the gray one in back of it—" He paused for her to listen. "—or if I turn them around like this?"

"Move the green one a little to the left, I say," she answered after due consideration. "Gives the music a little more bounce and babble."

Sooz smiled broadly. She could play this game, too. She rolled a boulder almost too heavy to lift into the water. She cocked her ear. "It just doesn't sound gurgly enough in this spot," she opined. She moved the rock closer to the others. "There, now, that's a real brook gurgle."

An hour of playful orchestration slipped by as fast as the water tumbling over the rocks, and the three, dripping wet and splotched with mud, sank in happy exhaustion on the creek bank to listen to their symphonic handiwork. The Singing Place had been restored.

"I can hear it better with my eyes closed," Sooz said. "I think the crick is singing 'Yankee Doodle Dandy.' "

"Maybe it's just talking. To the fish," Riley said. His eyes widened at his own imagination. "Maybe it's trying to tell *us* something."

"I think the crick is not actually singing," Sooz concluded. "Just humming."

"Well, I can't make out any distinct words or tunes," Grandmaw said, as seemingly serious as a school teacher. "I think maybe up at the first rapids, the words are *gurgly, gurgly, splash-bubbly splash*— repeated very fast at the second rapids: *gurglygurgly splashbubbly splash*."

They all tried to mimic the sound, repeating together as fast as their tongues would move:

Gurgly, gurgly,
Splashbubbly, splash.
Gurgly, gurgly,
Splashbubbly, splash.

To which Grandmaw threw in, the third time around:

Over the rocks,
The water flutes dash.

Which prompted Riley to chime in with:

And under the rocks,
The crawdaddies mash.

And Sooz, not to be outdone, added:

And around the rocks,
The little fish flash.

Their laughter joined with the creek's song, the two becoming a hymn of hope that every human could have a Singing Place if only—ah, if only—there were more Grandmaws as full of wonder and peace as the little children still are, in the quieter nooks of this poor, torn world.

About the Authors

Brenda Bayles is a writer and homesteader in Fredonia, Kansas.

Wendell Berry is the author of over thirty books of fiction, poetry, and essays, including *A Timbered Choir: The Sabbath Poems 1979–1997*. He writes and farms in Henry County, Kentucky.

Bill Duesing is an organic farmer and environmental artist. His collected essays are entitled *Living on the Earth*. He lives in Oxford, Connecticut.

Linda Egenes has written many *Plain* essays for young people, which she is gathering into a future book, *Visits with the Amish*.

John Taylor Gatto, New York State Teacher of the Year, garlic farmer, author of five books, including *Dumbing Us Down: The Hidden Curriculum of Compulsory Schooling*, and nationally acclaimed speaker, lives in New York City.

Art Gish is a former Brethren minister and current member of New Covenant Fellowship, a small Christian commune near Athens, Ohio. He is the author of *Beyond the Rat Race* and *Living in Christian Community*.

Seth Hinshaw works as a typesetter and printer. He is the clerk of Chesterfield Monthly Meeting of Friends and lives in Zanesville, Ohio.

James Huskins is a Brethren minister who farms in Marion, North Carolina.

David Kline is the author of *Great Possessions: An Amish Farmer's Journal* and *Scratching the Woodchuck: Nature on an Amish Farm*. He practices diversified farming on 120 acres in Holmes County, Ohio.

Mark Korban's family lives in his "still in process" strawbale house near Brownington, Vermont.

Mary Ann Lieser is a writer and mother living near Barnesville, Ohio. She is the managing editor of *Plain* magazine. Her work has appeared in *Coming Home*, *Plain*, and *Minutes of the Lead Pencil Club* (Bill Henderson, ed.).

Gene Logsdon is *The Contrary Farmer*, writer of over a dozen books and hundreds of magazine articles, and farmer of thirty acres in Wyandot County, Ohio. His latest book is entitled *You Can Go Home Again*.

Jerry Mander is a senior fellow at the nonprofit Public Media Center in San Francisco, program director for the Foundation for Deep Ecology, and chairperson of the International Forum on Globalization. He is the author of *Four Arguments for the Elimination of Television* and *In the Absence of the Sacred*. He coedited with Edward Goldsmith the groundbreaking book, *The Case Against the Global Economy*.

Jane Martin is the founder of The Natural Baby Company, where she pioneered mother-friendly employment policies. She lives in Trenton, New Jersey.

Franklin Saige is associate editor of *Plain* magazine and an unrecorded minister in the Religious Society of Friends. He lives east of Columbus, Ohio.

Scott Savage edits *Plain* magazine and is a cofounder of the Center for Plain Living. He organized the Second Luddite Congress in 1996 in Barnesville, Ohio, where he now resides.

Elmo Stoll lives in an Anabaptist community near Cookeville, Tennessee, and is a former editor of *Family Life*, the Amish magazine published in Ontario, Canada.

Chuck Trapkus lives and works at a Catholic Worker house in Rock Island, Illinois. He also edits and illustrates a newspaper, *The Catholic Radical.*

David and Elizabeth Vendley live in an Amish community in Marion, Michigan.

David Wagler is a member of the Old Order Amish church in Bloomfield, Iowa, and a retired bookstore owner. He is the author of several books, including *Stories behind the News*, as well as being a longtime "scribe" to *The Budget*, an Amish newspaper.